RED SOX ARE
THE CHAMPIONS
AFTER
86 YEARS

Finally

TRIUMPH
B O O K S

CHICAGO

The Boston Globe

This book is available in quantity at special
discounts for
your group or organization. For further in-
formation, contact:
Triumph Books
601 S. LaSalle Street
Suite 500
Chicago, Illinois 60605
Phone: (312) 939-3330
Fax: (312) 663-3557

Printed in the United States of America

TRIUMPH
B O O K S
CHICAGO

CREDITS

Editor Reid Laymance
Art director Rena Anderson Sokolow
Designer Tito Bottitta
Photo editor Jim Wilson
Photographers
Jim Davis (pages 7, 8, 18, 23, 26, 31, 37, 39, 41, 48, 50, 52, 53, 55, 59, 61, 62, 64, 67, 68, 70, 72, 74, 78, 80, 82, 89, 90, 95, 111)
Barry Chin (17, 18, 21, 28, 31, 38, 55, 56, 60, 69, 84, 85, 87, 99, 103)
Stan Grossfeld (3, 12, 14, 18, 34, 44, 46, 97)
John Bohn (27, 33)
David Kamerman (91)
Matthew J. Lee (90)
John Tlumacki (105, 112)
Michelle McDonald (109)
Justine Hunt (back cover)
Cover photo: Jim Davis

CONTENTS

By JACKIE MACMULLAN

Tears of joy

ST. LOUIS In a matter of 11 days, they turned the baseball world upside down. The Boston Red Sox, a franchise that had cornered the market on hardball heartache, that had shed too many tears and endured too many disappointments, vowed this time to alter history. ◆ The 2004 version of New England's most valued treasure, a happy bunch of idiots with flowing manes and sturdy bats, refused to buy into the myths that had burdened their predecessors. ◆ Instead, they found a way to write a new chapter in Red Sox lore, transforming themselves from frustrated losers on the brink of elimination to the finest of champions, laying claim to the most coveted prize in all of sports. ◆ A World Series ring. ◆ Go ahead. Say it. The Boston Red Sox have won the World Series. Let it roll off your tongue, washing away the bitter taste of 1948 and 1978 and 1986 and 2003. Let Bill Buckner and Mike Torrez and Grady Little go gracefully into the night. Let go of all the angst and anger and agony that has been simmering for 86 years. ◆ Revel in

this unorthodox group of athletes, who danced to their own beat, purists be damned. Marvel at their uncanny ability to rise from the ashes, and resurrect themselves in the most improbable of situations. No baseball team had come back from a 3-0 deficit to win a playoff series until the Red Sox pinned that indignity on their most hated rivals, the New York Yankees.

Seven days later, they completed a sweep of the St. Louis Cardinals, a team they dominated from the first pitch to the last, with a 3-0 victory in Game 4. After so many years of waiting, this Boston team made it look easy. Its pitcher, Derek Lowe, was superb. Its quirky center fielder, Johnny Damon, hit a leadoff homer last night to knock the Cardinals to where they had been from the beginning: on their heels. The Red Sox' defense, constructed with care at the cost of a former All-Star shortstop, was again reliable and comforting in the late innings.

There were times this ball club was infuriating, inconsistent, and undisciplined. The Sox were often questioned about their loose rules and long hair, but when it mattered most, they locked arms, banded together, and fulfilled the dreams of generations of crusty New Englanders.

"We did it, man," said Manny Ramirez, who nearly a year ago had so disheartened his employers he was put on waivers and went unclaimed. "I wish I was in Boston right now to celebrate with everyone." The unfamiliar surroundings of St. Louis did nothing to dampen the mood. There was first baseman Doug Mientkiewicz, skipping across the top of the Sox' dugout, celebrating with close to 1,000 Red Sox fans who refused to leave Busch Stadium. There was Curt Schilling, the most significant acquisition of the season, grabbing Jason Varitek by the shoulders and announcing, "Ladies and gentlemen, here is the leader of the 2004 Boston Red Sox." He then doused his catcher liberally with a double dose of Bud Light.

Varitek, so used to maintaining his businesslike visage, finally allowed himself to exhale and enjoy a moment he has been trying to orchestrate his entire career.

"I've been waiting seven years for this, but there are people in Boston who have been waiting a lot longer," he said. "It's such a relief for this to finally happen. As passionate as our fans are, they deserve this so much."

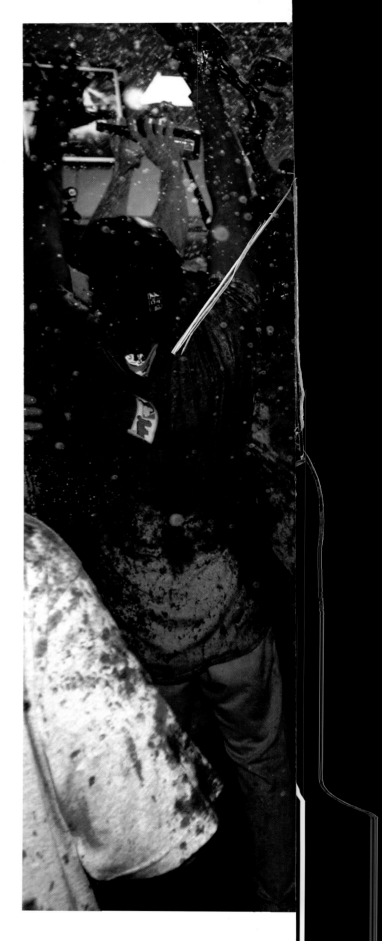

JOHNNY DAMON GETS A
WELL-DESERVED
CHAMPAGNE BATH

MANAGER TERRY FRANCONA AND GM THEO EPSTEIN EARNED THE RIGHT TO PARTY UNDER THE WATCHFUL EYES OF OWNERS LARRY LUCCHINO AND JOHN HENRY AFTER BRING-ING THE WORLD SE-RIES TROPHY HOME

The fantasy that New Englanders had been hoping for officially went into the books at 11:40 p.m., when Keith Foulke fielded Edgar Renteria's ground ball and gingerly tossed it to Mientkiewicz at first base. The Red Sox' dugout immediately emptied, with the players gathering at home plate and jumping up and down in unison, a victory scrum for a team that overcame nearly impossible odds.

"I'm still kind of in a daze," acknowledged right fielder Trot Nixon, who submitted three doubles in the clincher. "Did this really happen? I can only imagine what's going on back home right now."

More than one hour after the championship had been won, fans remained in this visiting ballpark, chanting "Thank You, Red Sox!" and "Papi, Papi!" in honor of the latest folk hero, David Ortiz. The Nation truly does extend across this country, as children as young as 2 years old wearing Red Sox garb toddled into the outfield as midnight approached. One woman, wearing the now signature "I believe!" jersey, admitted she was "over 82, that's all you need to know." She has been a Red Sox fan, she said, since she was old enough to have

"I've been waiting seven years for this, but there are people in Boston who have been waiting a lot longer," Jason Varitek said. "It's such a relief for this to finally happen. As passionate as our fans are, they deserve this so much."

a paper route to pay for tickets.

She grew to love this ragtag group for who they were: a freewheeling group that did not sweat the small stuff, and never took themselves too seriously. As Ramirez explained last night, "We always knew who we were. We never doubted who we were.

"Baseball is supposed to be fun. When you play that way, the game is easy. We found a way to make baseball easy."

Hard to imagine that 11 days ago, Kevin Millar would be filming his own home video version of "the greatest comeback in baseball history." Hard to imagine 11 days

ago that Lowe — how do you let this guy walk now? — was banished from the rotation, a lame-duck pitcher with no future in this town. Hard to imagine 11 days ago, Pedro Martinez's season, and perhaps his career with the Sox, was about to end in despair — again — against the Yankees.

Pedro hugged his manager, his teammates, his pitching coach, his trainer, his friend Ortiz. He doused his jeri curls with champagne and tears, only this time they were tears of satisfaction, and joy.

This time, the history of the Boston Red Sox had the very happiest of endings. ☺

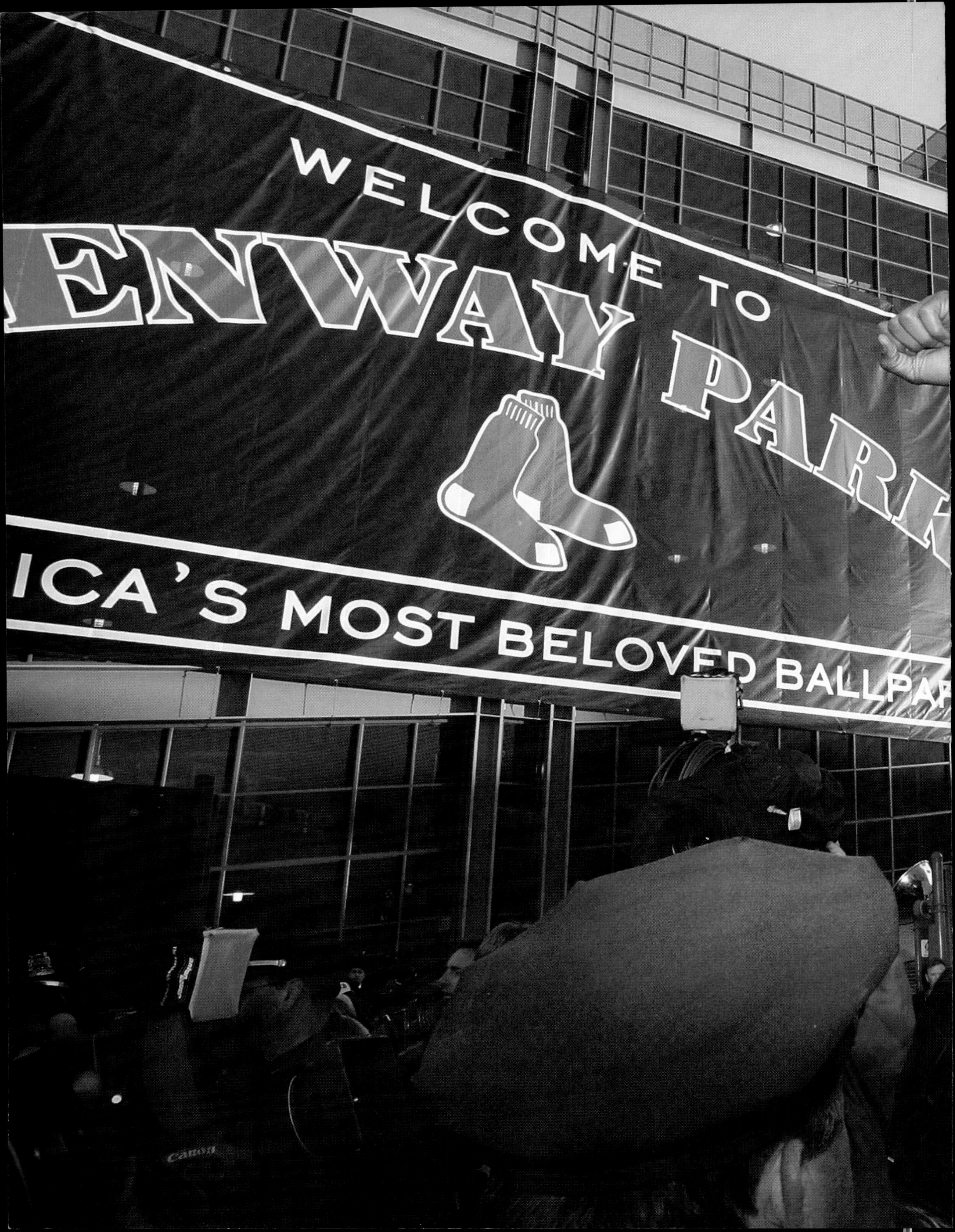
WELCOME TO
ENWAY PARK
ICA'S MOST BELOVED BALLPAR

FIRST PITCH
OCT. 23, 2004

Oh, Babe

ONCE UPON A TIME, Boston played in the World Series a lot and won them all – 1903, 1912, 1915, 1916 and 1918. But then came 1920 and the team sold Babe Ruth to the Yankees. The trips to baseball's Fall Classic changed. A loss in seven games to the Cardinals in 1946 when Enos Slaughter made his "mad dash" for home. A magical run to make the Series in 1967 only to fall to the Cards seven. Then came 1975 and Carlton Fisk's dramatic homer in Game 6 only to see the Reds win Game 7. In 1986, it was one out away from beating the Mets in Game 6. But in 2004 all that changed as Boston made a historic comeback to beat the Yankees in the ALCS and then swept the Cardinals in four.

1918

2004

By JACKIE MACMULLAN

Bellwether

BOSTON   You forget about Mark Bellhorn. He lulls you to sleep with those droopy eyes and that droopy hair and his insistence on examining every pitch as though it is a rare piece of art. He'll drive you crazy, this second baseman, who takes and takes and takes pitches until he either walks or strikes out.

Or hits incredible clutch home runs to win it.

While the St. Louis Cardinals were occupied with fretting about the lethal power of Manny Ramirez and David Ortiz, Boston's Pigpen second baseman, who was struggling so badly at the plate as recently as a week ago that Red Sox Nation was calling for his removal from the lineup, was quietly sizing up reliever Julian Tavarez in the bottom of the eighth.

The score recently had been tied on a pair of outfield errors by Ramirez, and this was a demoralizing thing, because the Sox had blown leads of 4-0, 7-2, and 9-7.

Even the Fenway Faithful couldn't help but look ahead to the top of the order for the kind of instant help that would be required to pull out this win. Maybe it was a rejuvenated Johnny Damon that could do it, or perhaps Manny, or the magical bat of David Ortiz. Bellhorn? It should have

occurred to them, but it didn't.

Bellhorn, meanwhile, quietly stepped into the box in the eighth, and quickly fell behind on the count, 1-2. Then, just like that, he swung the bat and lofted a shot to right field that clanged off Pesky's Pole for a two-run homer and an 11-9 lead that did hold this time.

For those of you scoring at home, the unassuming infielder now has hit home runs for the Red Sox in three consecutive postseason games. There was the critical — and unexpected — three-run blast off Jon Lieber in Game 6 of the ALCS against the Yankees that left disgruntled New Yorkers streaming for the exits muttering, "Mark 'Bleeping' Bellhorn." There was an insurance home run in Game 7 to clinch this World Series appearance.

And then there was the biggest hit of his life, a clanger off the pole that will join the annals of historic Red Sox home runs.

"I'm telling you something right now," said Kevin Millar. "That guy has been the unsung MVP for this team. The guy has been so awesome for this team. And he

STL	0	1	1	3	0	2	0	2	0	**9**	**11**	**1**
BOS	4	0	3	0	0	0	2	2	x	**11**	**13**	**4**

OCT. 23, 2004 • WILLIAMS VS WAKEFIELD

4

ERRORS BY THE
SOX, INCLUDING
ONE BY BRONSON
ARROYO
(TOP LEFT)

0

HITS BY ALBERT
PUJOLS (TOP
RIGHT) AND SCOTT
ROLEN, THE CARDS
3-4 HITTERS

5

OUTS RECORDED
BY KEITH FOULKE
(RIGHT) TO GET
THE SAVE

doesn't change his demeanor, no matter what's going on.

"We have never lost confidence in him. When all the TV people and the papers and the radio shows were on him, he was getting nothing but positive feedback from us here behind closed doors."

Bellhorn was getting more than that in the batting cages with hitting coach Ron Jackson. Papa Jack studied film of Bellhorn's swing during his horrendous 2-for-25 (.080) postseason start, which included 0 homers and 0 RBIs and enough strikeouts to wallpaper your kid's room.

"What we saw was his body was going around," Jackson reported. "You've got to keep your hands back, and stay on top of the baseball. He wasn't doing anything with his hands during that time. We spent a lot of time trying to make the adjustment.

"I'm so proud of him that he turned it around. And I give him a lot of credit. He and Johnny Damon were in that cage every day trying to work out their problems.

"The name of the game in the playoffs is making adjustments. You do that, and you're going to succeed."

As Damon and Bellhorn took extra swings, they talked about their futility, and the pressure to reverse their fortunes. Although Damon was struggling too, no one was calling for him to be yanked from the lineup. That was Bellhorn's lone cross to bear.

He's a tough kid," Damon said. "He's never had anything given to him. Sometimes you don't get a very good game from him, but guess what? He's always going to be prepared mentally and physically.

"I'm just so happy for him. He's a guy you just got to root for."

Sox manager Terry Francona was roundly criticized as Bellhorn continued to swing and miss, and his manager continued to pencil him into the lineup. His loyalty to his second baseman has been rewarded in the most crucial moments.

"If you watched him all year, you know he's a good player," said the manager. "He has a tendency to swing and miss. That's part of his game. He strikes out. But he's also hit a number of game-winning hits. I know myself, the coaching staff, and the other players feel real good about him. We feel like he's going to help us."

It will be accurate to say at this juncture that Bellhorn will not be sneaking up on the Cardinals for the rest of this series, not after submitting his winning blast, a second-inning single, and two walks. He is in his own kind of zone now, and Papa Jack says he can tell that his student is approaching pitchers with renewed aggressiveness.

"It's just confidence," Bellhorn explained. "I think we forget the mind is a powerful thing and sometimes we lose our confidence. You know, these games, you want to win them so bad that sometimes you put too much pressure on yourself and you start to struggle."

The struggles appear to be over. The hands are back, the average is up, and the hits just keep on coming. Yet Mark Bellhorn does not take this for granted. He has no illusions about replacing David Ortiz as the money man, or the home run king. For one night, the fantasy has come to life. If he has to go back to being a faceless, contributing second baseman, that's fine with him.

"Every little boy thinks of playing in the World Series and winning Game 7," Bellhorn said. "I know I did, I guess, but I'm not here trying to be a hero. I'm just trying to win four games."

One down, three to go.

Keith Foulke salvaged the victory by getting the final five outs. The Cardinals brought the tying run to the plate before Foulke got Yadier Molina to pop out and fanned Roger Cedeno.

"A lot of weird things happened in that inning," Foulke said of the eighth, "but you've got to get the job done. Obviously, it's going to be tough if we go out and play sloppy, but it was a weird game. It's probably not going to happen again."

While starting pitcher Tim Wakefield and the Sox' defense faltered, the mightiest offense in the game rescued them. Before Bellhorn struck, Señor Octubre, David Ortiz, led the way by launching a three-run shot in the first inning. Ramirez, despite his frolics in the field, helped by breaking out of his postseason RBI drought and knocking in a pair, including a go-ahead run to snap a 7-7 standoff in the seventh. Ortiz followed with a bad-hop single off Tony Womack's collarbone for a two-run lead.

Still, the Sox prevailed, as frightening as it was at times. ☻

STATISTICS

St. Louis

BATTER	AB	R	H	BI	AVG.
Renteria	4	1	2	1	.500
Walker	5	1	4	2	.800
Pujols	3	0	0	0	.000
Rolen	5	0	0	0	.000
Edmonds	4	2	1	0	.250
Sanders	3	1	0	0	.000
Womack	1	1	0	0	.000
Anderson	2	0	1	1	.500
Matheny	2	0	1	0	.500
Marquis pr	0	1	0	0	—
Molina	1	0	0	0	.000
Taguchi	3	1	1	0	.333
Cedeno ph	2	1	1	0	.500

PITCHER	IP	H	R	ER	ERA
Williams	2.1	8	7	7	27.00
Haren	3.2	2	0	0	0.00
Calero	0.1	2	2	2	54.0
King	0.1	0	0	0	0.00
Eldred	0.1	0	0	0	0.00
Tavarez (L)	1	1	2	1	9.00

Boston

BATTER	AB	R	H	BI	AVG.
Damon	6	1	2	1	.333
Cabrera	4	2	1	0	.250
Ramirez	5	0	3	0	.600
Ortiz	3	1	2	0	.667
Millar	5	1	1	1	.200
Mientkiewicz	0	0	0	0	—
Nixon	3	0	0	0	.000
Kapler ph	1	0	0	0	.000
Mueller	3	1	1	0	.333
Mirabelli	3	1	1	0	.333
Varitek ph	2	1	0	0	.000
Bellhorn	3	3	2	0	.667
Reese	0	0	0	0	—

PITCHER	IP	H	R	ER	ERA
Wakefield	3.2	3	5	5	12.27
Arroyo	2.1	4	2	2	7.71
Timlin	1.1	1	1	1	6.75
Embree	0	1	1	0	0.00
Foulke (W)	1.2	2	0	0	0.00

By JACKIE MACMULLAN

The big Schill

BOSTON Curt Schilling wasn't hedging on this. He wasn't thinking maybe, or I'm doubtful, or let's see. ◆ He was OUT. He was out as the Red Sox' Game 2 starter of the World Series. ◆ "I woke up at 7 o'clock in the morning,"

explained Boston's ace. "That was a tipoff right there. I've never woken up at 7 in the morning for anything in my life.

"I wasn't going to pitch. I couldn't walk. I couldn't move. I didn't know what happened, but I knew as soon as I woke up there was a problem."

His problem quickly became the problem of the Red Sox. Schilling was the automatic W. He was the one they were counting on to pin the St. Louis Cardinals against the Green Monster with a 2-0 Series deficit. He has been their most prolific, charismatic, and demonstrative player in this postseason, an almost mythical figure as he clawed his way through an ankle injury that will require surgery whenever this mystical, magical run is over.

The diagnosis was made long ago: a dislocated tendon that the Sox' medical staff sutured together for the critical ALCS Game 6 against the Yankees. When Schilling took the mound that night in Yankee Stadium a million years ago (seems that way, doesn't it?), nobody could have imagined a grittier, gutsier, or more inspiring

performance.

Compared to Game 2 of the World Series, that was nothing.

What Schilling submitted on a gray, cold, unforgiving night of baseball was truly unfathomable. He went from being unable to walk from his kitchen to his car to shutting down a Cardinals lineup that includes Jim Edmonds, Scott Rolen, and Larry Walker. He went from feeling more helpless than he's ever felt in his career to literally seizing this game and taking it over.

When Schilling trotted to the hill just after 8 p.m., the most surprised person in the park was his wife, Shonda, who had watched Schilling hobble into his car and back out of the driveway to give his baseball team the dreaded news.

"I told her it wasn't going to happen," he said. "There was no way. But that's when everything started. I left my house, and I'm driving to the park, and anyone who knows where Medfield is, they know it's a pretty long haul.

"There were signs every mile from my

OCT. 24, 2004 • SCHILLING VS MORRIS

"I woke up at 7 o'clock in the morning," explained Boston's ace. "That was a tipoff right there. I've never woken up at 7 in the morning for anything in my life.

THREE-FOR-ALL: GABE KAPLER, JOHNNY DAMON AND TROT NIXON CELEBRATE A WIN IN THE LAST GAME AT

house to this ballpark on fire stations, on telephone poles, wishing me luck. I can't explain what it was like.

"So I get here [to Fenway], and got out of the car, got into the trainer's room, and Doc [Bill Morgan] was there."

The Sox' medical staff examined Schilling and quickly determined an extra suture they had sewn in to provide some added stability to the area had nicked a nerve. As soon as that suture was re-moved, Schilling began experiencing auto-matic relief.

"And then it starts happening," Schilling said. "You start looking around at your teammates and understanding what you've been through over the past eight months, what it means to me.

"And then I did what I did the last time: I went to the Lord for help, because I knew, again, I wasn't going to be able to do this myself."

procedure never before performed on anyone except a cadaver.

Losing Schilling would have been a glancing blow to the Red Sox, who would have had to turn to Derek Lowe or Pedro Martinez, each of whom would have been pitching on three days' rest, to take the ball. It would have completely muddled the pitching rotation. It would have taken away the automatic W. It would have left them without their most potent pitcher.

It was a struggle for Curt Schilling last night, a struggle from the first fastball he fired past shortstop Edgar Renteria, to the final pitch that induced a grounder from Reggie Sanders in the sixth. His foot was numb, his mind was racing, and his hip flexor was tightening somewhere around the third inning.

He threw 24 pitches in that first inning, and 12 of them were to Renteria. It was exactly what the Red Sox had hoped to avoid, to put too much stress on Schilling too soon. Still, he escaped unscathed when Scott Rolen's screaming liner was snared by Bill Mueller.

Although trouble was lurking in almost every inning, Schilling was able to sidestep almost all of it. The Cardinals finally scored a run in the fourth, but it was unearned.

The Red Sox gave their starting pitcher plenty of run support (hey, it's the least they could do) to log this W. They will gladly do it again for him, provided there is a next time.

Can Schilling pitch again?

"I don't know," he admitted. "I haven't thought about it. I'm thinking about Pedro on the mound in St. Louis. I'm a little beat up right now. It's the first time in my life I've felt my age."

Schilling is 37. In all of those years, he never had a night like last night, when the impossible turned into the incredible.

"I wish everybody on this planet could experience the day I just experienced," he said. "I will never use the words unbelievable and the Lord again in the same sentence."

Schilling says he doesn't know if he could pitch again, but we do.

Of course he could. Haven't we learned anything?

Never — ever — count him out.

He's already had the ride of his life. ☺

As Mr. Curt's Wild Ride was unfolding throughout the day, his blissful fans knew nothing of his ordeal. All they knew was minutes before Game 2, Boston's prized pitcher was stalking — no, stalking would have been far too painful — let's say he was striding, back and forth to see if his sutured ankle could withstand another night of baseball. Nobody wanted to put pressure on the ace of this team, who already underwent a radical

STATISTICS

Boston

BATTER	AB	R	H	BI	AVG.
Damon	5	1	1	0	.250
O. Cabrera	4	1	2	0	.333
M. Ramirez	4	1	2	2	.462
D. Ortiz	4	0	1	0	.300
Mientkiewicz	0	0	0	0	-
Varitek	3	0	0	0	.125
Mueller	4	1	2	1	.500
Nixon	3	0	1	1	.200
Kapler ph	1	0	0	0	.000
Bellhorn	3	0	0	0	.333
Reese	0	0	0	0	.000
P. Martinez	2	0	0	0	.000
Millar ph	1	0	0	0	.143
Timlin	0	0	0	0	—
Foulke	0	0	0	0	—

PITCHER	IP	H	R	ER	ERA
Martinez (W)	7	3	0	0	0.00
Timlin	1	0	0	0	6.00
Foulke	1	1	1	1	2.25

St. Louis

BATTER	AB	R	H	BI	AVG.
Renteria	4	0	1	0	.273
L. Walker	3	1	1	1	.417
Pujols	4	0	1	0	.364
Rolen	3	0	0	0	.000
Edmonds	3	0	0	0	.091
R. Sanders	3	0	0	0	.000
Womack	3	0	0	0	.125
Matheny	2	0	0	0	.250
Cedeno ph	1	0	0	0	.333
Tavarez	0	0	0	0	—
Suppan	1	0	1	0	1.000
Reyes	0	0	0	0	—
M. Anderson	1	0	0	0	.200
Calero	0	0	0	0	—
King	0	0	0	0	—
Mabry	0	0	0	0	.000
Y. Molina	0	0	0	0	.000

PITCHER	IP	H	R	ER	ERA
Suppan (L)	4	8	4	4	7.71
Reyes	0	0	0	0	0.00
Calero	1	1	0	0	13.50
King	2	0	0	0	0.00
Tavarez	1	0	0	0	4.50

By BOB HOHLER

Magic #1

ST. LOUIS A day after the 18th anniversary of Bill Buckner's fateful error in Game 6 of the 1986 World Series, the Red Sox knew they were battling history as well as the Cardinals, even as the folks back home planned a historic victory parade.

"Every time I see that ground ball rolling through the guy's legs, I turn the channel," first baseman Doug Mientkiewicz said. "I don't want to see that. It plays in your mind."

After all, the Sox seized a 2-0 lead on the road against the Mets in the '86 Series before misery befell them in seven games after Buckner's blunder. And the last thing Terry Francona's dream-chasers wanted to do after going up, 2-0, in the 2004 Series was give the Cardinals a chance to tarnish another fine Boston player's legacy. As deposed manager Grady Little said after last year's disastrous finish against the Yankees in the American League Championship Series, some of his players feared becoming the next Buckner.

Fear not.

Hardball heaven is one step away after Pedro Martinez and the Sox exploited the blundering Cardinals and banked a 4-1 victory before 52,015 at Busch Stadium to build a 3-0 cushion in the 100th Fall Classic.

No team has blown a 3-0 lead in the World Series, but the Sox were not silly enough to place their faith in the historical record, especially after they became the first team in history to overcome a 3-0 deficit when they stunned the Yankees in the ALCS.

As if Martinez had something to prove — he made his World Series debut and perhaps his last start in a Boston uniform — he capitalized on the Cardinals running into two devastating outs in the first three innings and silenced the tailspinning Redbirds through seven.

"It's been a great ride," said Martinez, who is eligible for free agency after the Series. "I hope everybody enjoyed it as much as I did.

"I hope I get another chance to come back with this team, but I understand the business part of it. I hope everybody understands that I'm not the one who wanted to leave. If they don't get me, it's probably because they didn't try hard enough. My heart is with Boston."

Twice Martinez ran into trouble and

BOS	1	0	0	1	2	0	0	0	0	**4**	**9**	**0**
STL	0	0	0	2	0	0	0	0	1	**1**	**4**	**0**

OCT. 26, 2004 • MARTINEZ VS SUPPAN

14

BATTERS RETIRED IN A ROW BY PEDRO MARTINEZ

18

HOME RUNS IN THE POST-SEASON BY MANNY RAMIREZ, SECOND ALL-TIME

21

TEAMS TO HAVE TAKEN A 3-0 LEAD IN A WORLD SERIES

LARRY WALKER IS OUT AT THE PLATE ON A THROW BY MANNY RAMIREZ AND A TAG BY JASON VARITEK

each time the Cardinals rescued him. First, Larry Walker tried to score on a bases-loaded fly to left with one out in the first inning, only for Manny Ramirez to gun him down at the plate. Then with none out and runners at second and third in the third inning, old friend Jeff Suppan committed one of the ugliest gaffes in postseason history and ran himself into a rally-killing double play.

You could almost hear grateful New Englanders murmur, "Thanks, guys."

"It was a break," Martinez said, "and we took advantage of it."

With a little help from the Cardinals, Martinez made himself a winner by surrendering only three hits and a pair of walks. He retired the final 14 batters he faced after Suppan's blunder and capped his performance by catching Reggie Sanders swinging at a 92-mile-per-hour fastball to end the seventh.

"Phenomenal performance," Curt Schil-

ling said. "He was unbelievable. They had one shot and they missed, and he ran with it after that."

The Sox bullpen handled the rest, as Mike Timlin retired the Cardinals in order in the eighth and Keith Foulke finished them off in the ninth despite surrendering his first run of the postseason, a one-out solo homer by Larry Walker.

"One more win!," a throng of Sox fans chanted behind the dugout afterward.

Ramirez set the tone for the Sox offense by launching a solo homer off Suppan in the first inning and singling home another run in the fifth. Trot Nixon and Bill Mueller also chipped in with RBI singles.

"This is big, but we learned our lesson against the Yankees," Ramirez said. "The Cardinals have such a great team. You've got to keep grinding out until you win the last game."

The Sox became the 21st team in World Series history to grab a 3-0 lead. Of the first

20 teams, all but three swept the Series.

Things got dicey again for Martinez in the third. Suppan started it by legging out an infield hit leading off. Edgar Renteria followed with an opposite-field double to the warning track in right, sending Suppan to third.

But once again fortune smiled on the Sox in their moment of need. Walker bounced a routine grounder to second baseman Mark Bellhorn, who was prepared to allow Suppan to score from third. Bellhorn fired to first to retire Walker, but in a crucial blunder, Suppan ran halfway for home, only to reverse direction, prompting David Ortiz to throw to Mueller at third in time to double up Suppan and kill the rally.

La Russa said Suppan misheard his orders from third base coach Jose Oquendo.

"Jeff heard, 'No, no,'" La Russa said, "and he was yelling, 'Go, go,'" The Sox gathered momentum as Mueller doubled to left-center with two out in the fourth inning and raced home on Nixon's single deep to right for a 2-0 lead. And they struck again in the fifth when Ramirez singled home Johnny Damon, who had doubled leading off against Suppan, and Mueller knocked in Orlando Cabrera, who had singled.

"We're playing hard, but we still have another game," Cabrera said. "It ain't over till we win."

STATISTICS

Boston

BATTER	AB	R	H	BI	AVG.
Damon	5	1	1	0	.250
O. Cabrera	4	1	2	0	.333
M. Ramirez	4	1	2	2	.462
D. Ortiz	4	0	1	0	.300
Mientkiewicz	0	0	0	0	-
Varitek	3	0	0	0	.125
Mueller	4	1	2	1	.500
Nixon	3	0	1	1	.200
Kapler ph	1	0	0	0	.000
Bellhorn	3	0	0	0	.333
Reese	0	0	0	0	.000
P. Martinez	2	0	0	0	.000
Millar ph	1	0	0	0	.143
Timlin	0	0	0	0	—
Foulke	0	0	0	0	—

PITCHER	IP	H	R	ER	ERA
Martinez (W)	7	3	0	0	0.00
Timlin	1	0	0	0	6.00
Foulke	1	1	1	1	2.25

St. Louis

BATTER	AB	R	H	BI	AVG.
Renteria	4	0	1	0	.273
L. Walker	3	1	1	1	.417
Pujols	4	0	1	0	.364
Rolen	3	0	0	0	.000
Edmonds	3	0	0	0	.091
R. Sanders	3	0	0	0	.000
Womack	3	0	0	0	.125
Matheny	2	0	0	0	.250
Cedeno ph	1	0	0	0	.333
Tavarez	0	0	0	0	—
Suppan	1	0	1	0	1.000
Reyes	0	0	0	0	—
M. Anderson	1	0	0	0	.200
Calero	0	0	0	0	—
King	0	0	0	0	—
Mabry	0	0	0	0	.000
Y. Molina	0	0	0	0	.000

PITCHER	IP	H	R	ER	ERA
Suppan (L)	4	8	4	4	7.71
Reyes	0	0	0	0	0.00
Calero	1	1	0	0	13.50
King	2	0	0	0	0.00
Tavarez	1	0	0	0	4.50

JEFF SUPPAN'S BASE-RUNNING BLUNDER COST THE CARDINALS A CHANCE TO SCORE

BOS	1	0	2	0	0	0	0	0	0	3 9 0
STL	0	0	0	0	0	0	0	0	0	**0** 4 0

OCT. 27, 2004 • LOWE VS MARQUIS

17

LEAD-OFF HOME
RUNS IN WORLD
SERIES HISTORY,
THE LATEST BY
JOHNNY DAMON
(TOP LEFT)

3

DOUBLES BY
TROT NIXON
(TOP RIGHT)
IN GAME 4 TO
DRIVE IN THE
OTHER TWO RUNS

11–3

BOSTON'S RECORD
IN POST-SEASON
PLAY, FOURTH-
BEST IN HISTORY

By BOB HOHLER

Finally...

ST. LOUIS Hail the lovable idiots. Bless the baseball gods. Raise a cup to the good souls in Red Sox lore —from Ted Williams and Joe Cronin to Gary Waslewski and Pumpsie Green — who chased but never captured the game's greatest prize. ◆ The Red Sox are champions of the world. ◆ Avengers of 86 years of raw yearning, Terry Francona's raggedy renegades liberated generations of Sox fans from the purgatory of their unrequited dreams when they buried the Cardinals, 3-0, before 52,037 under a canopy of clouds beneath a Blood Red Moon at Busch Stadium to win their first World Series since 1918. ◆ "All the waiting and all the great faith they have finally paid off in the end," principal owner John W. Henry said amid a sudsy celebration for the ages in the Sox' clubhouse. "It took us a while but we got it done." ◆ Whatever it was — a drought, a curse, a confluence of misfortune and mismanagement that endured longer than Soviet communism and doctors making house calls — it's over. The end came on the 18th anniversary of their last great heartache, losing the '86 Series to the Mets. ◆ "This is for

4

SAVES FOR KEITH
FOULKE (TOP
LEFT) AGAINST
THE CARDINALS

5

CONSECUTIVE
GAMES IN WHICH
THE RED SOX
SCORED FIRST

8

CONSECUTIVE
WINS IN THE
POST-SEASON,
A RECORD

champs

anyone who ever played for the Red Sox, anyone who ever rooted for the Red Sox, anyone who has ever been to Fenway Park," said general manager Theo Epstein, the kid from Brookline, Mass., who grew up to build a champion. "This is bigger than the 25 players in this clubhouse. This is for all of Red Sox Nation past and present. I hope they're enjoying it as much as we are." ◆ Party on, New England. At 11:40 p.m. EDT, the Sox returned to the pinnacle of the national pastime when Keith Foulke retired Edgar Renteria for the final out to complete a spectacular four-game sweep of a St. Louis team that posted the best record in the majors (105-57) in the regular season. ◆ The historic triumph touched off a delirious celebration from the infield in St. Louis to the far reaches of New England. While the Sox jumped all over each other in joy, great-grandparents who were old enough to remember Babe Ruth helping the Sox win their last World Series and star-struck school children whose memories run little deeper than the Manny Era reveled back home. ◆ "Thank you, Red Sox!" hundreds of fans chanted nearly

3

CLINCHING
WINS FOR DEREK
LOWE IN THE
POST-SEASON

1

RUN ALLOWED BY
THE RED SOX
BULLPEN AGAINST
THE CARDINALS

17

CONSECUTIVE
GAMES IN WHICH
MANNY RAMIREZ
GOT A HIT
IN THE
PLAYOFFS

an hour after the game as the celebration spilled back onto the field.

All across America, the Sox of yesteryear smiled along, from the '46 teammates to the classes of '67, '75, and '86, whose broken dreams the freewheeling boys of '04 fulfilled. One of the elder statesmen, Johnny Pesky, joined in the clubhouse celebration.

One and all, they could thank the resurgent Derek Lowe for helping them across the threshold. Cast aside in early October, Lowe returned by mid-month to pitch the clincher of the American League Division Series against the Angels, win Game 7 of the Championship Series against the Yankees, and shine in the biggest challenge of his career as he silenced the Cardinals for seven innings to triumph in the World Series finale.

"I can't wait till next year when we go back to Yankee Stadium and don't have to hear that 1918 chant anymore," Lowe said. "There were a lot of guys who fought for this organization for a lot of years and never won. I hope they enjoy this because they're part of history."

The affable sinkerballer became the first pitcher in history to win the clinchers of three postseason series in the same year.

"It's going to hit home probably in a week when we go home and settle into our own houses and realize what we just did," Lowe said after pitching perhaps his last game in a Sox uniform.

The Sox captured their sixth world championship — and swept their first World Series — after Johnny Damon got them rolling by launching a home run off Jason Marquis leading off the game. Trot Nixon (three doubles in four at-bats) provided the rest of the production by doubling home two runs in the third inning.

"A lot of people thought it would never happen," Damon said, "so to be able to celebrate and carry that trophy, that's what it's all about."

Lest there be any doubt about the enormity of their resurgence, Henry, one of the most brilliant number-crunchers in high finance, crunched the numbers on the eve of their elimination game against the Yankees. By his calculations, the chances of the Sox escaping the ALCS jam were 6.25 in 100.

"Pretty damn bad," he said in layman's terms.

Then the Sox stuck the Cardinals in a similar hole, forcing them to try to become the first team since the 1970 Orioles to play a fifth game after dropping the first three of a World Series. And the Cards got no help from Lowe, who surrendered only three hits and a walk over seven scoreless innings in a performance as masterful as his two predecessors, Pedro Martinez and Curt Schilling.

"We're world champions," Schilling said. "There's no living player who can say what we can say today: We're the world champion Boston Red Sox."

Schilling won his second World Series ring, Martinez his first.

"The ring is meaningless, it's a material thing," Martinez said. "But the feeling that the people are going to have in Boston is indescribable."

As efficient as he was effective, Lowe fired only 85 pitches over seven innings before he yielded to a pinch hitter, Kevin Millar, in the eighth. Millar had a chance to break the game open with the bases loaded and none out, but he struck out before Damon bounced into a fielder's choice, erasing Bill Mueller at the plate, and Orlando Cabrera struck out to end the threat.

With Lowe gone, Bronson Arroyo got the first out in the eighth inning before he walked pinch hitter Reggie Sanders. Francona summoned Alan Embree, who caught pinch hitter Hector Luna swinging at a 94-mile-per-hour heater and retired Larry Walker on a weak pop to short.

Foulke, the most valuable addition to the team this year other than Schilling, did the rest, finishing off the Cardinals for the fourth time in as many games.

The Sox never trailed in the Series, becoming the first team to lead from start to finish in a World Series since the 1966 Orioles against the Dodgers (the '89 Giants never led against the A's but tied them once).

The Sox worked the magic partly by feasting on the Cards in the first inning, as they did at times against the Yankees. Thanks to Damon's homer, the Sox scored in the first inning for a fifth straight postseason game and for the sixth time in their seven playoff games. The shot also marked the fourth time in the last five games the Sox homered in the first inning.

Damon's homer was the 17th leading

Boston

BATTER	AB	R	H	BI	AVG.
Damon	5	1	2	1	.286
O. Cabrera	5	0	0	0	.235
M. Ramirez	4	0	1	0	.412
D. Ortiz	3	1	1	0	.308
Mientkiewicz	1	0	0	0	.000
Varitek	5	1	1	0	.154
Mueller	4	0	1	0	.429
Nixon	4	0	3	2	.357
Bellhorn	1	0	0	0	.300
Lowe	2	0	0	0	.000
Millar ph	1	0	0	0	.125

PITCHER	IP	H	R	ER	ERA
Lowe (W)	7	3	0	0	0.00
Arroyo	0.1	0	0	1	6.75
Embree	0	0	0	0	0.00
Foulke (S)	1	1	0	0	1.80

St. Louis

BATTER	AB	R	H	BI	AVG.
Womack	3	0	1	0	.182
Luna ph	1	0	0	0	.000
Walker	2	0	0	0	.357
Pujols	4	0	1	0	.333
Rolen	4	0	0	0	.000
Edmonds	4	0	0	0	.067
Renteria	4	0	2	1	.333
Mabry	3	0	0	0	.000
Isringhausen	0	0	0	0	—
Molina	2	0	0	0	.000
Cedeno	1	0	0	0	.250
Matheny	0	0	0	0	.250
Marquis	1	0	0	0	.000
Anderson	1	0	0	0	.167
Haren	0	0	0	0	—
Sanders	0	0	0	0	.000
Reese	1	0	0	0	.000

PITCHER	IP	H	R	ER	ERA
Marquis (L)	6	6	3	3	3.86
Haren	1	2	0	0	0.00
Isringhausen	2	1	0	0	0.00

KEITH FOULKE AND DOUG MIENTKIEWICZ MAKE THE FINAL OUT FOR THE CHAMPIONSHIP

off a first inning in World Series history and the first since Derek Jeter hit one for the Yankees in Game 4 of the 2000 Subway Series against the Mets. The last Sox player to homer leading off the first inning in a World Series was Patsy Dough- erty in Game 3 of the 1903 Series against the Pirates.

"I'm sure there are a lot of people in New England who are dancing in the streets right now," Francona said. "For that, I'm thrilled." ⚾

By BOB HOHLER

Fits & starts

NEW YORK File under: Things gone wrong. ◆ No one said Curt Schilling would be, well, Curt Schilling at his best when he carried the hopes of Red Sox fans to the mound at Yankee Stadium. Everyone knew he

suffered from tendinitis behind his right ankle and needed an injection of the numbing agent Marcaine simply to pitch.

But Schilling and the Sox hoped against hope he would be fine. They conducted a test run at Fenway Park and all parties involved — Schilling, manager Terry Francona, general manager Theo Epstein, and medical director Bill Morgan — saw no reason to push back his start.

As it turned out, Schilling needed more time to heal before he faced the Yankees in the crucial opener of their best-of-seven American League Championship Series.

What now?

In an injury-shortened outing that raised questions about how effective he may be the rest of the way, Schilling survived only three stressful innings as the Yankees thumped him for six runs en route to a 10-7 victory before 56,135 on 161st Street. On the night Schilling hoped to "shut up" the sellout crowd, he instead endured the ignominy of the masses chanting, "Who's your daddy?"

"The bell rang and I couldn't answer it," Schilling said, acknowledging that the in-

jury prevented him from generating the power he needed to drive off the mound. "I've been looking forward to this for almost a year, so it's very disappointing, but it's one game and it's over."

The only consolation was a rousing comeback attempt in which the Sox weathered 6⅓ perfect innings from Yankee starter Mike Mussina to close within 8-7 and bring the go-ahead run to the plate in the eighth. Even after they fell behind, 10-7, in the eighth, the Sox put the tying run at the plate in the ninth before Bill Mueller grounded into a game-ending double play against Mariano Rivera.

"It was a tough game to lose," Manny Ramirez said, "but at least we let them know we can come back at any time."

The question is, will Schilling's injury prevent him from coming back in the series? He said he would know more about his condition today and declined to speculate on whether he could make his next scheduled start in Game 5, if necessary.

"If I can't go out there with something better than what I had today, I'm not going back out there," he said. "This is

		1	2	3		4	5	6		7	8	9		R	H	E
BOS		0	0	0		0	0	0		5	2	0		**7**	**10**	**0**
NY		2	0	4		0	0	2		0	2	x		**10**	**14**	**0**

OCT. 12, 2004 • SCHILLING VS MUSSINA

THE YANKEES HAD
CURT SCHILLING
SCRATCHING HIS
HEAD WITH SIX RUNS
IN THREE INNINGS

not about me braving through something. This is about us and winning the world championship, and if I can't give them better than I had today, I won't take the ball again."

The outing was Schilling's shortest — other than a game in 2001 that was suspended because a light transformer exploded in San Diego — since May 22, 1997, when he lasted only 2⅔ innings for the Phillies against the Mets. And he could be forgiven for the brevity of the '97 outing because he went sleepless the night before as he stayed up with his wife, Shonda, who delivered their daughter, Gabriella, at 6:30 a.m. This time it was Schilling rather than Shonda who needed medical attention after the Yankees torched him for two runs in the first inning and four more in the third as he struggled to hit 90 on the radar gun. Rarely exceeding 86 to 87, he surrendered six hits, including a three-run double to Hideki Matsui, and a pair of walks before the Sox mercifully lifted him.

After Schilling's struggles, Francona dismissed as premature a question about whether the Sox may need to replace Schilling with Derek Lowe for Game 5. Francona seemed encouraged that Schilling "didn't complain about any pain or anything like that."

Still, some of Schilling's teammates harbored some concern.

"It is a concern?" Alan Embree said. "You've got to think so, but you don't know with the treatment and the attention he gets from the doctor. It helps. We'll have to wait and see."

With Schilling long gone, the Sox finally got to Mussina when Mark Bellhorn broke up his bid for a perfect game by driving an 0-and-2 pitch to the warning track in left-center for a one-out double. A batter later, David Ortiz singled Bellhorn to third, setting the stage for three consecutive run-scoring hits: a two-run double by Kevin Millar, an RBI single by Trot Nixon, and a two-run homer by Jason Varitek.

Varitek's homer, off Tanyon Sturtze, was his eighth in postseason play.

"We showed a lot of fight to come back in that game," Varitek said.

The Sox made it even more interesting in the eighth inning when Ortiz tagged Tom Gordon for a two-run triple — he narrowly missed a home run — to lift the Sox within a run, 8-7, before the Yankees summoned Rivera, just returned from attending the funeral of relatives who died at the swimming pool at his home in Panama.

Bernie Williams also helped to spoil Boston's comeback attempt by ripping a two-run double over Ramirez in left field in the eighth off Mike Timlin, giving the Yankees a three-run cushion with three outs to go. Alex Rodriguez and Gary Sheffield stroked consecutive singles off Timlin to set up the crusher by Williams.

"It was a tough play," Ramirez said. "I just missed it."

"It was just one game," Ramirez said. "We're going to keep battling." ☻

THE YANKEES HAD MANNY RAMIREZ ON THE RUN AS HE CHASES DOWN A DOUBLE BY BERNIE WILLIAMS

STATISTICS

Boston

BATTER	AB	R	H	BI	AVG.
Damon	4	0	0	0	.000
Bellhorn	4	1	1	0	.250
M. Ramirez	4	1	1	0	.250
D. Ortiz	4	1	2	2	.500
Millar	4	1	1	2	.250
Nixon	4	1	1	1	.250
Varitek	4	1	2	2	.500
O. Cabrera	4	0	1	0	.250
Mueller	4	1	1	0	.250

PITCHER	IP	H	R	ER	ERA
Schilling (L)	3	6	6	6	18.00
Leskanic	1	0	0	0	0.00
Mendoza	1	1	0	0	0.00
Wakefield	1	3	2	2	18.00
Embree	1	1	0	0	0.00
Timlin	0.2	2	2	0	27.00
Foulke	0.1	0	0	0	0.00

New York

BATTER	AB	R	H	BI	AVG.
Jeter	4	1	1	0	.250
Rodriguez	5	2	2	0	.400
Sheffield	4	4	3	0	.750
Matsui	5	2	3	5	.600
B. Williams	5	0	2	3	.400
Posada	3	0	0	1	.000
Olerud	3	0	1	0	.333
Cairo	4	0	1	0	.250
Lofton	3	1	1	1	.333

PITCHER	IP	H	R	ER	ERA
Mussina (W)	6.2	4	4	4	5.40
Sturtze	0.1	1	1		27.00
Gordon	1.2	3	2	2	27.00
M. Rivera (S)	1.1	2	0	0	0.00

MARIANO RIVERA SAVED THE GAME FOR NEW YORK AFTER RETURNING HOME FROM A FUNERAL IN PANAMA

By GORDON EDES

Double dip

NEW YORK Maybe it will seem just mere whistling in the Bronx, these pledges by manager Terry Francona and general manager Theo Epstein even before Boston's 3-1 loss in Game 2 that the Red Sox would somehow find a way to overcome the possible loss of Curt Schilling for the rest of this American League Championship Series because of a torn tendon in his right ankle.

With Jon Lieber doing a passable impression of Mike Mussina, holding the Sox to three hits and a run through 7 innings plus in outdueling Pedro Martinez, and Mariano Rivera starring again as his incomparable self, the Sox last night were placed in dire peril of having this season end like the 85 that have preceded it. Since the LCS went to a best-of-seven format in 1985, 15 teams have taken a 2-0 series lead, and all but two have advanced to the World Series, including

2

BOS	0 0 0	0 0 0	0 1 0	**1 5 0**
NY	1 0 0	0 0 2	0 0 x	3 7 0

OCT. 13, 2004 • MARTINEZ VS LIEBER

MANNY RAMIREZ
AND THE SOX WERE
AT A LOSS AGAINST
JON LEBER

the last 13 in a row.

As if the Sox, of all teams, needed any more history lessons. If they don't start hitting - they went down 19 in a row to start Game 1 and managed just two base runners in the first six innings last night — they may all find themselves under a mango tree, to borrow an allusion from Martinez, who was down, 1-0, three batters into the game and was ultimately done in by a two-run home run in the sixth by John Olerud, who had a chance to come to Boston this summer after being released by the Seattle Mariners but never called back.

In a heartfelt but remarkably offbeat aside, Martinez said he not only wasn't dismayed by the "Who's your daddy?" chants that filled the Bronx last night, the ones he'd invited by assigning paternity to the Yankees after they'd beaten him in Boston last month, but actually enjoyed them.

"It actually made me feel really, really good," he said. "I don't know why you guys laugh. It really made me feel really important. When I think where I was 15 years ago, sitting under a mango tree without 50 cents to pay for a bus, and today I was the center of attention for the entire city of New York. I don't regret one bit [what I said]."

For all the attention he received last night, however, the Yankees appear bent on rendering the Sox obsolete, sooner than later after Lieber held them to three singles until departing after allowing Trot Nixon's base hit to open the eighth. Setup man Tom Gordon entered and gave up a double to Jason Varitek and a run-scoring groundout by Orlando Cabrera. Gordon also retired Bill Mueller for the inning's second out, before Joe Torre summoned Rivera, who caught Johnny Damon (0 for 8, 5 K's

ORLANDO CABRERA DIDN'T HAVE ANY WORDS OF ADVICE FOR PEDRO MARTINEZ, WHO TOOK THE LOSS

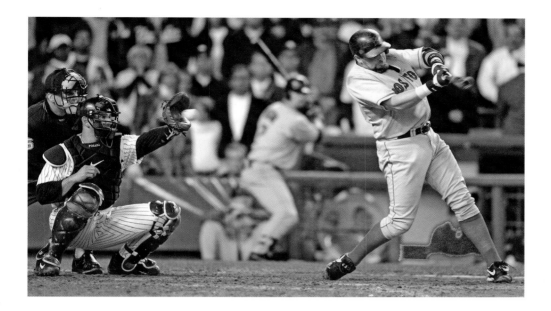

STATISTICS

Boston

BATTER	AB	R	H	BI	AVG.
Damon	4	0	0	0	.000
Bellhorn	4	0	0	0	.125
Ramirez	4	0	1	0	.250
Ortiz	3	0	1	0	.429
Millar	4	0	0	0	.125
Nixon	3	1	1	0	.286
Varitek	3	0	1	0	.429
Cabrera	3	0	1	1	.286
Mueller	3	0	0	0	.143

PITCHER	IP	H	R	ER	ERA
Martinez (L)	6	4	3	3	4.50
Timlin	0.2	1	0	0	13.50
Embree	0.2	2	0	0	0.00
Foulke	0.2	0	0	0	0.00

New York

BATTER	AB	R	H	BI	AVG.
Jeter	3	1	0	0	.143
Rodriguez	4	0	1	0	.333
Sheffield	4	0	2	1	.625
Matsui	4	0	1	0	.444
Williams	4	0	0	0	.222
Posada	2	1	1	0	.200
Olerud	4	1	1	2	.286
Cairo	2	0	0	0	.167
Lofton	4	0	1	0	.286

PITCHER	IP	H	R	ER	ERA
Lieber (W)	7	3	1	1	1.29
Gordon	0.2	1	0	0	13.50
Rivera (S)	1.1	1	0	0	0.00

KEVIN MILLAR, STRIKING OUT, AND THE SOX WERE QUIET AT THE PLATE AGAIN

in the LCS) looking at a called third strike). In the ninth, Rivera struck out David Ortiz and Kevin Millar after Manny Ramirez's one out double to close out the Sox.

During the regular season, the Sox have shown Rivera to be vulnerable - he's blown five saves against them since the start of the 2002 season. But in the postseason, he's 6 for 6 in save opportunities against the Sox, including saves in the first two games here.

"I think we had some poor at-bats," Varitek said. "We got ourselves out. Pedro pitched very well. We just didn't do the job on our end."

The Sox have no illusions about the task ahead of them.

"We've been in tough situations before," said Sox closer Keith Foulke, who has been rendered a bit player in these last two games, "and we've shown that we're very capable of coming back. We've gotten ourselves in a hole, and now we've got to go home and climb out of it."

Jeter, who walked, stole second and scored the Yankees' first run on Gary Sheffield's single, is not assuming anything.

"Winning two is great," he said, "but it doesn't mean anything if we don't win two more."

Francona, who may not be able to call upon Schilling to pitch again in this series after the severity of his injury was revealed, had bravely vowed that the Sox would forge ahead without him.

"If we're not able to overcome some adversity, whether it's Schill getting beat in Game 1, if that's all it ends up being, which we're hopeful, or if it ends up being more than that, if we are not able to overcome it, we're not a good enough team," he said before Game 2. I don't think anybody in that clubhouse, including myself, thinks that that's the case."

Epstein summoned similar words in Francona's office after appearing with Sox medical director William Morgan to inform the world that Schilling, who had envisioned shutting up 55,000 Yankee fans, might instead have to shut down because of a torn ankle tendon.

"This is the same bunch of guys who lost their starting shortstop [Nomar Garciaparra] and starting right fielder [Nixon] in spring training and had a great April, and then overcame more adversity in the middle of the season," said Epstein.

"We can win this series with Curt or without Curt. It will be a greater challenge without him. We battled these guys down to the last at-bat last season with John Burkett in that slot. Burkett is a heck of a pitcher, but you know what I'm saying. We can still win this series. That's our plan."

After the game, it was more of the same.

"The last time we were here, however long ago it was, I remember saying something about the Yankees putting us in their rearview mirror, but I thought we would fight our way back and we did," said Francona." ☺

RAIN DAY

BRONSON ARROYO
AND THE SOX GOT
AN EXTRA DAY OFF
THANKS TO RAIN
THAT DAMPENED
FENWAY AND
PUSHED GAME 3
BACK A DAY

By BOB HOHLER

Home wreckers

BOSTON Religious leaders prayed for the Red Sox to reach baseball's promised land. The mayor appealed for divine intervention. Even comic Jim Dunn led the congregants at the Comedy Connection last night in a prayer service.

So why did the Sox all but find themselves on death's postseason doorstep? Why was a team that opened the playoffs with such extraordinary promise one loss away from receiving last rites?

Blame the baseball gods, if it helps ease the heartache.

But the fact is, there may be too little ink in the newspaper's printing plant to list the ways the Sox turned a night of mighty hope into a calamitous collapse of the worst order as Terry Francona's crew suffered a historically embarrassing 19-8 defeat to the Yankees and plunged into a 3-0 chasm in the best-of-seven American League Championship Series before a stunned 35,126 at Fenway Park.

"It was just a [butt]-kicking all the way around," starter Bronson Arroyo said, after putting the Sox on the path to the horrible finish. "You would try to forget about

it during the regular season, but to get destroyed like this when it's crunch time and have a football score up there at the end of the game, it's definitely embarrassing."

No team has come back from a 3-0 deficit in postseason history. And the Yankees have not lost four straight games since April 22-25, when they dropped the finale of a road trip in Chicago and were swept in a three-game series by the Sox in the Bronx.

The watchword for the Sox by the end of the rout was "desperate." As in, very desperate.

"We have to do what's never been done in history," Johnny Damon said, "and that's come back from a 3-0 deficit."

In a humiliating performance that set an array of records for pitching futility in a League Championship Series, Arroyo and five relievers were punished unre-

NY	3 0 3	5 2 0	4 0 2	**19 22 1**
BOS	0 4 2	0 0 0	2 0 0	**8 15 0**

OCT. 16, 2004 • BROWN VS ARROYO

ONLY FENWAY
FAITHFUL REMAINED
AFTER THE YANKEES
SET AN AMERICAN
LEAGUE RECORD
WITH 19 RUNS

THE SCOREBOARD ON THE GREEN MONSTER SAID IT ALL AS NEW YORK HAD AN ANSWER FOR EVERY SOX RALLY

lentingly as the ugliness unfolded over the longest nine-inning game (4 hours, 20 minutes) in postseason history.

"We had a night where none of our pitchers located, I mean none of them," Francona said. "We walked guys, we hit some guys, we gave up a lot of extra-base hits. That's a bad combination."

The Yankees set a record for the LCS with the 19 runs and matched a record for hits (22) set by the Braves in 1996.

They also matched the record for doubles (eight).

"It's like they have a certain gear right now," Damon said. "They're playing the best we've seen them play all year. It wasn't fun."

It got so bad that Francona was forced to summon his projected Game 4 starter, Tim Wakefield, who fared nearly as badly as Arroyo. By using Wakefield to try to stop the bleeding, the Sox left themselves

"It's going to be a tough road for us," Wakefield said. "It's never fun being down, 3-0, but I think everybody in this clubhouse is still optimistic."

The Sox will go nowhere but home for the winter if Lowe fails to overcome the demons that turned Arroyo and Co. into a veritable crew of batting practice hurlers. The Yankees rolled up a 13-6 lead by the fifth inning and never let up as they peppered the Fens with a dizzying barrage of hits, including home runs by Hideki Matsui (a two-run shot off Arroyo and another off Mike Myers), Alex Rodriguez (a solo blast off Arroyo), and Gary Sheffield (a three-run jack off Curtis Leskanic).

Rodriguez, Sheffield, Matsui, and Bernie Williams combined to go 16 for 22 (.727), score 14 runs, and knock in 15.

"It's a pretty potent lineup over there," Wakefield said. "I don't know why it happened the way it happened. It was one of those nights where no matter what we threw up there, they found holes and got hits. They were just better than we were, that's for sure."

The Sox entered the game knowing they needed to score runs to salvage their waning season after their 3-1 loss in Game 2 in the Bronx. In their urgency, they scored six in a hurry as they routed Yankees starter Kevin Brown after two innings and slapped around his successor, Javier Vazquez, for a couple more.

But the Sox pitched so miserably that many of the fans who adore them turned on them, showering them with boos and catcalls, before they all but abandoned them. In an eerie sight, the stands were as empty as they have been all season by the eighth inning of New York's runaway victory.

It was horrible," Arroyo said. "We dug ourselves as big a hole as you can dig yourself, but we have to keep fighting to dig our way out of it. What else are you going to do?'

"We figured we would be the ones ahead, 3-0," Damon said. "But they're doing exactly what we thought we would be doing."

Not to worry, Francona said.

"It was disappointing for everybody, but we're not done," he said. "I fully expect we'll come out [tonight] and play our [butts] off." ☺

little choice but to tap Derek Lowe, their Game 5 starter, to pitch Game 4 and try to keep alive their fleeting chance of advancing to their first World Series in 18 years and ending their 86-year championship drought.

Should they prevail tonight, the Sox would tap Pedro Martinez for Game 5, then pray to the baseball gods who spurned them to deliver Curt Schilling from his ankle injury.

STATISTICS

New York

BATTER	AB	R	H	BI	AVG.
Jeter ss	4	2	1	0	.182
Rodriguez	5	5	3	3	.429
Sheffield	5	3	4	4	.692
Crosby pr	0	1	0	0	—
Matsui	6	5	5	5	.600
Williams	6	1	4	3	.400
Posada	5	1	2	1	.300
Sierra	6	0	2	2	.333
Olerud	4	0	0	0	.182
Clark	2	0	0	0	.000
Cairo	4	1	1	0	.200

PITCHER	IP	H	R	ER	ERA
Brown	2	5	4	3	13.50
Vazquez (W)	4.1	7	4	4	8.31
Quantrill	1.2	2	0	0	0.00
Gordon	1	1	0	0	7.71

Boston

BATTER	AB	R	H	BI	AVG.
Damon	5	1	1	1	.077
Bellhorn	4	0	0	0	.083
Ramirez	4	0	1	0	.250
Ortiz	5	1	3	0	.500
Varitek	3	3	2	2	.500
Mirabelli	1	0	0	0	.000
Nixon	5	1	2	2	.333
Millar	5	1	1	0	.154
Mueller	4	1	2	0	.273
Cabrera	4	0	3	2	.455

PITCHER	IP	H	R	ER	ERA
Arroyo	2	6	6	6	27.00
Mendoza (L)	1	1	1	1	4.50
Leskanic	0.1	3	3	3	20.25
Wakefield	3.1	5	5	5	14.54
Embree	0.1	2	2	2	9.00
Myers	2	5	2	2	9.00

Game time

4 hrs. 20 mins.

By BOB HOHLER

Fenway spark

BOSTON This was the year. Manny Ramirez said so and everyone believed him, it seemed, even the oddmakers. ◆ This was the year, the Sox maintained, even after they dropped the first two games of the American League Championship Series against the Yankees.

"We can change history," the message said on their clubhouse door. "Believe it."

Maybe only the Derek Lowes of the world recognized the inherent danger of buying into the October hype that the Sox would capture the franchise's first world championship in 86 years.

"Oddsmakers, schmoddsmakers," Lowe said on the eve of the series. "That means absolutely nothing."

So it was that Lowe, an uncharacteristic voice of reason whose days in Boston almost certainly are numbered, found himself carrying the franchise's imperiled hopes to the

NY	0 0 2	0 0 2	0 0 0	0 0 0	**4 12 1**
BOS	0 0 0	0 3 0	0 0 1	0 0 2	6 8 0

OCT. 17, 2004 • HERNANDEZ VS LOWE L L L W

DAVID ORTIZ ENDED ANOTHER LONG NIGHT AT FENWAY ON A HAPPIER NOTE WITH A TWO-RUN HOMER IN THE TWELFTH

mound as the Sox trailed the Yankees, 3-0, in the best-of-seven series. Lowe knew the numbers as well as anyone: No team in baseball history had rallied from a 3-0 deficit to win a best-of-seven series, and 20 of the 25 teams that previously had seized a 3-0 lead swept Game 4.

But, wait. Make that 20 sweeps in 26 tries as the Sox staged a sensational come-from-behind victory, rallying from a 4-3 deficit in the ninth inning to force extras before David Ortiz struck a dramatic two-run homer in the 12th in a 6-4 thriller before a frenzied 34,826 at Fenway Park to save their season.

Ortiz went deep off the fifth Yankee pitcher, Paul Quantrill, after Ramirez sin-

gled leading off the inning.

Curtis Leskanic, who got the last out of the 11th with the bases loaded and held off the Yankees in the 12th, picked up the win.

"We're 3-1 right now, but you never know what can happen," said Ortiz. "We're going to continue trying to win. This is a team that never gives up. We've had a whole bunch of games coming behind like that."

After the longest game in ALCS history (5 hours, 2 minutes), baseball lives another day in Boston. No bubbly just yet for the Yankees in the musty little bandbox on Yawkey Way. Pedro Martinez goes in Game 5 tonight for the Sox in the Fens as he tries to send the series back to the Bronx with

Curt Schilling poised to start Game 6.

Oddsmakers, schmoddsmakers.

Trailing, 4-3, in the ninth, Kevin Millar launched the ninth-inning rally to keep the Sox alive by drawing a leadoff walk off Rivera. He yielded to pinch runner Dave Roberts, who promptly stole second. One pitch later, Bill Mueller stunned Rivera for the second time this season, ripping a 93-mile-per-hour cutter up the middle to knock in Roberts, tie the score, and spoil Rivera's save opportunity (Mueller also clubbed a walkoff homer off Rivera in the July 24 classic at Fenway).

"There's not too many guys who can do that against Mariano," Leskanic said. "It was a huge lift for our ball club."

At that, Doug Mientkiewicz, pinch hitting for Mark Bellhorn, sacrificed Mueller to second before first baseman Tony Clark muffed a slow roller by Johnny Damon for an error, putting runners at the corners.

Rivera got a huge out by fanning Orlando Cabrera on three pitches, then walked Ramirez to load the bases. But Ortiz ended the threat by popping out to second, forcing extra innings.

The rally helped the Sox extend their last-gasp bid to spare themselves from spending the winter remembered as architects of one of the most stunning collapses in team history. They knew if their comeback bid failed the Sox brass would begin by the close of business today setting a course for 2005, a year likely of new faces and the same old dreams. Fifteen of the Sox are eligible for free agency after the World Series. ☺

By GORDON EDES

Marathon men

BOSTON No, Doug Mientkiewicz said, he wasn't the first Red Sox player to reach David Ortiz after another swing of Ortiz's big bat once again brought deliverance, and another day, to a season that refuses to end, bookend wins of historic length over the New York Yankees in a span of less than 24 hours.

"I ran out there," Mientkiewicz said, "but I had to get Johnny's hair out of my face."

Johnny Damon's hair will flow at least one more night, and the Red Sox will be in the Yankees' faces for at least another game, after Ortiz ended the longest game in postseason history with a 14th-inning single off Esteban Loaiza, the seventh Yankee pitcher of the night, giving the Sox a 5-4 win in Game 5 of the American League Championship Series. The victory came on the same day that Ortiz's walkoff home run (at 1:22 a.m.) had beaten the Bombers in Game 4, and it staved off elimination for the second straight game.

"Every time you just say, almost in the back of your head, gosh, it's physically impossible for him to do it again," Mientkiewicz said of Ortiz's winning hit, his third of this postseason, these two against the Yankees joining his walkoff 10th-inning home run that eliminated Anaheim in the Division Series. "It's just not that easy. To continually do it night in and night out, it's ridiculous. It's a freak of nature."

The Sox, the 26th team to fall behind, 3-0, in the postseason, are attempting to become the first to overcome that deficit to win the series. Sox manager Terry Francona said Curt Schilling, despite a torn tendon in his right ankle, will start Game 6 in Yankee Stadium, wearing a Bill Buckner-like black boot specially designed for the ace. Can the Sox do the unthinkable?

"We're in the same position as last year," said Sox owner John W. Henry, noting that the Sox trailed, three games to two, when they returned to New York in the ALCS last year, "and we came awfully close. But the odds are still against us."

Of Paul Revere, JFK, and Ortiz,

| | | NY | 0 1 0 | 0 0 3 | 0 0 0 | 0 0 0 | 0 0 | **4** | **12** | **1** |
| | BOS | 2 0 0 | 0 0 0 | 0 2 0 | 0 0 0 | 0 **1** | **5** | **13** | **1** |

OCT. 18, 2004 • MUSSINA VS MARTINEZ L L L W W

PEDRO MARTINEZ (TOP RIGHT) STARTED BUT COULDN'T FINISH; KEITH FOULKE (MIDDLE RIGHT) WAS PERFECT AGAIN; MARIANO RIVERA (BOTTOM) BLEW ANOTHER SAVE; AND TIM WAKEFIELD WAS THERE FOR THE WIN

18

NUMBER OF
RUNNERS
THE YANKEES LEFT
IN SCORING
POSITION

226

NUMBER OF
PITCHES THROWN
BY SEVEN
RED SOX
PITCHERS

where does Ortiz rank in New England's affections?

"It's not even close," Henry replied.

Game 5 lasted 5 hours 49 minutes — 47 minutes longer than the 5:02 the teams played the night before.

"It's Groundhog Day," said Yankees manager Joe Torre, whose team had won seven straight Game 5s and 11 of 13 since the start of the 1996 postseason, but fell on a night they left 18 runners on base and went 1 for 13 with runners in scoring position. "I'll take nominations and I might be in sort of a haze, but I think that was one of the greatest games ever played, if not the greatest," said Red Sox general manager Theo Epstein after a game that started with Pedro Martinez in danger of losing once again to the Bombers – Derek Jeter's three-run, bases-clearing double in the sixth had given the Yanks a 4-2 lead— but ended with six Sox relievers holding the Yankees scoreless for the final eight innings on five hits.

Tim Wakefield, who was supposed to have started Game 4 but instead has come out of the bullpen three times in this series, was credited with the win after holding the Yankees to one hit in the final three innings, and escaping a Yankee threat in the 13th that began with Gary Sheffield reaching on a third-strike Jason Varitek passed ball and ended with Ruben Sierra striking out on a full-count knuckleball with runners on second and third after two more passed balls.

"I just tried to keep us in the game as long as possible," said the gallant Wakefield. "I didn't know how many innings I would be able to go. After the second inning, they asked me how I felt and I said, 'I'll give you what I got.'"

Ortiz, who had singled home the Sox' first run in the first inning, then homered in the eighth off Tom Gordon when the Sox erased a 4-2 deficit and sent the game into extra innings, ended a 10-pitch at-bat against Loaiza by lining a soft single well

DAVID ORTIZ
ENDED ANOTHER
ONE WITH A
RUN-SCORING
SINGLE IN THE
FOURTEENTH

in front of center fielder Bernie Williams. The hit scored Damon, who is battling his worst slump of the season (2 for 24) but drew a one-out walk and took second on a full-count, two-out walk to Manny Ramirez, who has not driven in a run in five games of this ALCS, matching the longest stretch in which he has not knocked in a run this season.

"That was phenomenal, and one of the best at-bats I've ever seen to end it," Epstein said. "Loaiza was throwing nuclear stuff out there and locating. But David was so locked in, and to foul all those balls off the way he did and then to hit that ball to center was remarkable."

Mariano Rivera is widely considered history's greatest closer; in 65 postseason appearances, Rivera never had blown consecutive save opportunities, having converted 32 of 36 chances. But the Sox got to Rivera in the bottom of the ninth in Game 4, on Bill Mueller's RBI single after Dave Roberts stole second, and again last night, when Rivera was brought into a nigh-inescapable situation in the bottom of the eighth. Gordon, who already had allowed Ortiz's homer to make it 4-3, put runners on the corners when he walked Kevin Millar and Trot Nixon hit a run-and-hit single to center, sending pinch runner Roberts to third. Rivera gave up a sacrifice fly to Varitek, who hit a ball deep enough to center field, and the score was tied.

Through nine innings, the Yankees left 14 men on base and were 1 for 10 with runners in scoring position. The most glaring failure came in the eighth, when the Yankees, up, 4-2, blew a great chance after Miguel Cairo's leadoff double off reliever Mike Timlin and Jeter's sacrifice bunt. Alex Rodriguez went down swinging against Timlin, and after a walk to Gary Sheffield, Terry Francona brought in Keith Foulke, who had thrown 50 pitches in working 2 2/3 innings in Game 4. Foulke retired hot-hitting Hideki Matsui on a liner to left, keeping it close for the Sox to rally in the bottom of the inning.

The Sox had gone 19 up, 19 down against Mike Mussina in Game 1 before Mark Bellhorn's double with one out in the seventh spoiled the bid for perfection. Last night, they made Mussina uncomfortable from the outset, as first-inning singles by Orlando Cabrera, Ramirez, and Ortiz brought home one run, and a bases-load-

ed, two-out walk to Varitek, batting right-handed against Mussina, made it 2-0.

The Sox had runners at first and second on a base hit by Ramirez and a one-out error by Jeter, who booted Millar's ground ball, but Mussina struck out Nixon and Varitek on a total of six pitches.

The Yankees finally broke through against Martinez in the sixth, with the kind of good fortune that last month led Martinez to suggest that the Yankees were his "daddy." With one out, Posada hit a chopper over Martinez's head for a base hit, the ball seeming to veer away from a charging Cabrera. Sierra then lined a single to center — Posada stopping at second while the Yankee bench screamed at him to take third on the weak-armed Damon. Martinez caught Clark looking at a full-count cutter for the second out, but hit Cairo in the front shoulder with a 1-and-0 fastball, loading the bases. Up came Jeter, who had been dreadful (0 for 3, two whiffs, an error) to that point. He sliced a ball that landed just inside the right-field line for a double that cleared the bases, Cairo beating Nixon's throw and Varitek's tag.

When Martinez then hit A-Rod in the elbow with a pitch, many in the crowd of 35,120 — mindful that Martinez's pitch count had eclipsed 100 — yelled for Francona to lift the Dominican ace (a couple of spectators practically leaned into the dugout to make their case). Francona, hands in the pockets of his jacket, was unmoved, even as Martinez walked Sheffield to load the bases. His faith in Martinez was rewarded — barely — as Nixon made a sliding catch of Matsui's screamer.

Bellhorn's double to open the seventh was the end for Mussina. Torre went to Worcester's Tanyon Sturtze, the 6-foot-5-inch righthander. Sturtze retired Damon on a pop to short but walked Cabrera in a nine-pitch at-bat.

Torre went to the pen again for Gordon to face Ramirez. Ramirez could not deliver, grounding into an around-the-horn double play despite a bone-crushing attempt by Cabrera to break it up with a hard slide into Cairo.

But leading off the eighth Ortiz, who is making a case for being Boston's greatest October performer of all time, homered into the Monster seats to cut the lead to 4-3. It was only a hint of what was to come. ☺

STATISTICS

New York

BATTER	AB	R	H	BI	AVG.
Jeter	7	0	1	3	.182
Rodriguez	4	0	0	0	.304
Sheffield	4	0	0	0	.409
Matsui	7	0	1	0	.444
B. Williams	7	1	2	1	.321
Posada	6	1	2	0	.350
Sierra	5	1	3	0	.412
T. Clark	7	0	1	0	.200
Cairo	6	1	2	0	.250

PITCHER	IP	H	R	ER	ERA
Mussina	6	6	2	2	4.26
Sturtze	0.1	0	0	0	3.38
Gordon	0.2	2	2	2	7.20
Rivera	2	1	0	0	1.35
Heredia	0.1	1	0	0	0.00
Quantrill	1.0	2	0	0	6.75
Loaiza (L)	3.1	1	1	1	2.70

Boston

BATTER	AB	R	H	BI	AVG.
Damon	6	1	1	0	.083
Cabrera	6	1	2	0	.348
Ramirez	6	0	2	0	.333
Ortiz	6	2	3	3	.478
Millar	2	0	0	0	.176
Roberts pr	0	1	0	0	—
Mientkiewicz	2	0	1	0	.333
Nixon	4	0	1	0	.238
Kapler pr	2	0	0	0	.000
Varitek	4	0	0	2	.263
Mueller	6	0	1	0	.273
Bellhorn	6	0	2	0	.150

PITCHER	IP	H	R	ER	ERA
Martinez	6	7	4	4	5.25
Timlin	1.2	2	0	0	6.75
Foulke	1.1	1	0	0	0.00
Arroyo	1	0	0	0	18.00
Myers	0.1	0	0	0	7.71
Embree	0.2	1	0	0	4.15
Wakefeld (W)	3	1	0	0	8.59

Game time
5 hrs. 49 mins.

By BOB HOHLER

Reversal of fortune

NEW YORK Baseball players become heroes only if they risk their lives for noble causes, like Ted Williams in the Korean War. ◆ So don't even think about hailing Curt Schilling and the amazin' Red Sox as heroes. But what-

ever you call them, make it special because Terry Francona's band of history-defying rogues last night reached the threshold of the unfathomable.

Rising from the ashes of an ankle injury that will require surgery within 48 hours of his season ending, Schilling carried his teammates with him as the Sox stunned the Yankees, 4-2, in Game 6 of the American League Championship Series last night and became the first team in baseball history to surge back from an 0-3 deficit in a best-of-seven series and force a Game 7.

Amazin'.

"We just did something that has never been done," Schilling said. "It's not over yet by any stretch."

They may not be heroes, but Boston's boys of October remarkably continued their quest to "change history" and play

another night. Derek Lowe was the projected starter for Game 7 tonight as the Sox bid for their first World Series berth in 18 years.

"We have a chance to shock the United States of America," Kevin Millar said.

Cancel Wednesday night Bingo. It's winner-take-all tonight in the Bronx.

While Schilling did what he failed to do in Game 1 — "make 55,000 people from New York shut up" at Yankee Stadium — the often-ridiculed Mark Bellhorn scored a giant measure of redemption by slugging a three-run homer off Jon Lieber in the fourth inning to give the Sox all the runs they needed to advance to Game 7.

"It's my first time being involved in something like this," said Bellhorn, who was hitting .143 (3 for 21) in the series when he stepped to the plate. "Sometimes you try too hard, but my teammates kept

BOS	0 0 0	4 0 0	0 0 0	**4**	**11**	**0**
NY	0 0 0	0 0 0	1 1 0	**2**	**6**	**0**

OCT. 19, 2004 • SCHILLING VS MUSSINA   L L L W W W ◇

CURT SCHILLING,
PITCHING WITH
STITCHES IN HIS
RIGHT ANKLE, HELD
THE YANKEES
TO ONE RUN IN
SEVEN INNINGS

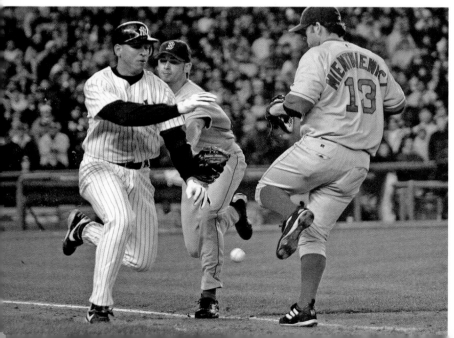

pumping me up. For me to do something like this, it's pretty big for me."

Schilling, pitching with a shot of the painkiller Marcaine after he underwent a minor surgical procedure Monday on the dislocated tendon in his right ankle, man-handled the Yankees for seven innings, al-lowing a lone run on four hits, including a solo homer by Bernie Williams. Schil-ling lacked his overpowering fastball but his command was superb in his 99-pitch work of magic. He walked none and struck out four before he handed off to Bronson Arroyo, who allowed a run in the eighth before Keith Foulke survived a scare in the ninth.

"It was definitely inspiring," Johnny Da-mon said of Schilling's comeback. "He had someone looking down on him so he could go seven innings, and he knows it. He's very proud."

Foulke, who already had pitched four times in the series and was appearing in his third game in as many nights, walked two batters to bring the winning run to the plate with two outs before he fanned old friend Tony Clark to complete the sen-sational comeback.

Schilling to Foulke: Just as the Sox pic-tured it last winter when they acquired the two stars to try to improve on last year's finish, five outs shy of a trip to the World Series.

"The fact that [Schilling] went so deep made the eighth easier for Bronson and we got to Foulke where we didn't have to extend him more than one inning," Fran-cona said. "It gives us a chance to have some guys fresher [tonight]."

And all the game took was 3 hours and 50 minutes, a sprint by the marathon standards of the previous three.

In the history of Major League Base-ball, the NBA, and the NHL, 230 teams have fallen behind, 3-0, in a best-of-seven series, and only two hockey teams — the '42 Maple Leafs and '75 Islanders — have come back and won.

But none of the 25 baseball teams that failed were anything like the '04 Sox, a self-described "bunch of idiots" who rebound-

UMPIRES CALLED ALEX RODRIGUEZ FOR INTERFERENCE AFTER KNOCKING THE BALL OUT OF BRONSON ARROYO'S GLOVE

MARK BELLHORN, DROPPED TO NINTH IN THE BATTING ORDER, RESPONDED WITH A THREE-RUN HOMER FOR THE WIN

STATISTICS

Boston

BATTER	AB	R	H	BI	AVG.
Damon	5	0	1	0	.103
Mueller	4	0	0	0	.231
Ramirez	4	0	1	0	.320
Ortiz	4	0	0	0	.407
Nixon	3	0	0	0	.208
Kapler ph	1	0	1	0	.333
Millar	4	1	2	0	.238
Mientkiewicz	0	0	0	0	.333
Varitek	4	1	3	1	.348
Cabrera	4	1	2	0	.370
Bellhorn	3	1	1	3	.174
Reese pr	0	0	0	0	.000

PITCHER	IP	H	R	ER	ERA
Schilling (W)	7	4	1	1	6.30
Arroyo	1	2	1	1	15.75
Foulke (S 1)	1	0	0	0	0.00

New York

BATTER	AB	R	H	BI	AVG.
Jeter	4	0	1	1	.192
Rodriguez	4	0	1	0	.296
Sheffield	4	0	1	0	.385
Matsui	3	0	0	0	.400
Williams	4	1	1	1	.313
Posada	4	0	0	0	.292
Sierra	3	0	0	0	.350
Clark	4	0	0	0	.158
Cairo	3	1	2	0	.304

PITCHER	IP	H	R	ER	ERA
Lieber (L)	7.1	9	4	4	3.14
Heredia	0.1	0	0	0	0.00
Quantrill	0.2	0	0	0	5.40
Sturtze	0.2	0	0	0	2.70

ed from one of the worst embarrassments in postseason history (a 19-8 pounding in Game 3) to push the Yankees to the limit. The Sox did it with pitching, timely hitting, and an infield that has not committed an error in eight postseason games.

Arroyo momentarily was charged with an error when things got ugly in the Bronx with the Sox leading, 4-2, five outs from victory. After Derek Jeter singled home Miguel Cairo, who had doubled with one out in the eighth inning, Alex Rodriguez rolled a dribbler toward first base. Arroyo fielded the ball and tried to tag Rodriguez, who slapped at Arroyo's glove and sent the ball hurtling into foul territory, allowing Jeter to race home.

First base ump Randy Marsh initially ruled Rodriguez safe, which would have meant the Yankees had a runner on second, one out, and a 4-3 score. But after Francona protested, the umpires powwowed and reversed the ruling, calling Rodriguez out for interference. Jeter returned to first with two outs. The decision sent the crowd into an angry frenzy, as spectators pelted the field with balls, plastic bottles, and beer cups, briefly prompting the Sox to retreat to their dugout as venerable PA announcer Bob Sheppard appealed for order. Once peace was re-

stored, Arroyo got Gary Sheffield to pop out to snuff the threat.

But the crowd continued to clamor, prompting police to line the first and third base lines and the area near the Sox dugout where team executives were seated with officers in riot-control gear — another dark, memorable image in the ancient rivalry.

As for Schilling, he picked the time of his life to post his first career win in Yankee Stadium (he was 0-2 with a 7.11 ERA in four previous appearances). And Lieber was no match for him, as Damon set the tone for the Sox offense by waging a 10-pitch struggle leading off the game. Though Damon fanned, he signaled that the Sox would challenge Lieber, unlike Game 2, when they went quietly as Lieber tossed only 82 pitches over seven-plus innings. They forced him to throw 124 in 7 1/3 innings last night.

Millar got things started against Lieber in the fourth inning doubling to the base of the wall in the left-field corner. Lieber responded by getting ahead of Varitek, 0-and-2, before he wild-pitched Millar to third and found himself in a mighty struggle with Varitek. The 10-pitch at-bat ended with Varitek rifling a single to center to knock in Millar with the first run. ☺

POLICE STATE

AFTER YANKEE FANS GOT RESTLESS WHEN SEVERAL CALLS WENT AGAINST NEW YORK, THE CITY'S POLICE SQUAD LINED THE FIELD FOR THE FINAL INNING

7

BOS	2	4	0	2	0	0	0	1	1	**10**	**13**	**0**
NY	0	0	1	0	0	0	2	0	0	**3**	**5**	**2**

OCT. 21, 2004 • LOWE VS BROWN

IT WAS A GRAND NIGHT FOR JOHNNY DAMON, WHO HIT A GRAND SLAM IN THE SECOND INNING

By BOB HOHLER

A miracle

NEW YORK Just like that, they shocked the nation. Just as they pictured it, they changed the course of baseball history. And just like a dream, they dashed generations of heartache for New Englanders who longed to witness the one glorious triumph they staged last night in the October chill by the Harlem River. ◆ In the greatest postseason comeback since the birth of the national pastime, the Red Sox completed a magical surge from a 3-0 deficit in the best-of-seven American League Championship Series by stomping the Yankees, 10-3, in a do-or-die seventh game to capture their first pennant since 1986. ◆ "How many times can you honestly say you have a chance to shock the world?" Kevin Millar said in the frothy celebration after the sensational finish. ◆ "It might happen once in your life or it may never happen. But we had that chance, and we did it. It's an amazing storybook."

DEREK LOWE,
PITCHING ON TWO
DAYS REST, PUT
THE YANKEES
OUT FOR THE REST
OF THE SEASON

STATISTICS

Boston

BATTER	AB	R	H	BI	AVG.
Damon	6	2	3	6	.171
Bellhorn	3	1	1	1	.192
Reese	0	0	0	0	.000
Ramirez	5	1	1	0	.300
Ortiz	4	1	1	2	.387
Varitek	5	0	1	0	.321
Nixon	5	1	1	0	.207
Millar	3	1	1	0	.250
Mientkiewicz	1	0	1	0	.500
Mueller	4	1	2	0	.267
Cabrera	2	2	1	1	.379

PITCHER	IP	H	R	ER	ERA
Lowe (W)	6	1	1	1	3.18
Martinez	1	3	2	2	6.23
Timlin	1.2	1	0	0	4.76
Embree	0.1	0	0	0	3.86

New York

BATTER	AB	R	H	BI	AVG.
Jeter	4	0	1	1	.200
Rodriguez	4	0	0	0	.258
Sheffield	4	0	0	0	.333
Matsui	4	1	2	0	.412
Williams	4	1	1	1	.306
Posada	3	0	0	0	.259
Lofton	3	0	1	1	.300
Clark	2	0	0	0	.143
Olerud ph	1	0	0	0	.167
Sierra ph	1	0	0	0	.333
Cairo	2	1	0	0	.280

PITCHER	IP	H	R	ER	ERA
Brown (L)	1.1	4	5	5	21.60
Vazquez	2	2	3	3	9.95
Loaiza	3	4	0	0	1.42
Heredia	0.2	0	0	0	0.00
Gordon	1.2	3	2	2	8.10
Rivera	0.1	0	0	0	1.29

ALEX RODRIGUEZ, ONCE COURTED BY THE RED SOX, WAS HITLESS IN GAME 7

Forget the fall foliage romps this weekend. The 100th World Series opens Saturday night at Fenway Park as the Sox face the Astros or Cardinals in the quixotic quest for their first world championship since 1918.

"We still have another hill to climb," Sox president and CEO Larry Lucchino said. "We don't want to forget that in the euphoria of the moment."

Thanks to a magnificent start on two days' rest by Derek Lowe and a big-bang attack led by Johnny Damon, series MVP David Ortiz, and Mark Bellhorn, the Sox became the first team in baseball history to come back from a 3-0 deficit to win a best-of-seven series. Four straight nights the champagne chilled in the Yankee clubhouse, and four straight nights the Sox dodged elimination, marking the first time in 14 years a Boston team beat the Pinstripers four times in as many days.

"How can this not be one of the greatest comebacks in the history of sports?" Sox principal owner John W. Henry said. "This team loves each other so much. They want to win so badly for one another and they wanted to win so badly for these fans. There's no way you can do this unless you have incredible heart."

The Sox won the franchise's 11th AL pennant in a wondrous twist in a journey that began 243 days earlier when they gathered for spring training to avenge last year's heartbreaking loss in Game 7 of the ALCS to the Yankees. But they also scored sweet revenge for forebears such as Johnny Pesky and Bobby Doerr, who lost the final two games of the 1949 season to the Yankees with the pennant on the line, and

Jim Rice and Dwight Evans, who watched Bucky "Bleeping" Dent's home run ruin their chances for a division title in a one-game division playoff in 1978.

"There have been so many great Red Sox teams and players who would have tasted World Series champagne if it wasn't for the Yankees," general manager Theo Epstein said. "Guys in '49, '78, and us last year. Now that we've won, this is for them. We can put that behind us and move on to the World Series and take care of that."

A preschooler in 1978, Lowe looked like an ace last night as he whipsawed the Yankees over six innings, allowing only one run on one hit (RBI single by Derek Jeter), a walk, and a hit batsman, completing his personal comeback from exiled starter when the playoffs opened to team savior.

"Games like this make or break your so-called career," Lowe said. "I know a lot of people in Boston have been talking about this whole free agency thing and keep saying this is going to be your last game. Luckily, it's not going to be."

While Lowe all but silenced a Yankee juggernaut that exploded for 19 runs in humiliating the Sox in Game 3, Damon staged his own remarkable reversal of fortune. He entered the game batting .103 with one RBI in the first six games of the series, still burdened by his role in the first three losses. But nearly four months after he took Yankees righthander Javier Vazquez deep twice in a game in the Bronx June 29, Damon struck again, launching a grand slam off Vazquez in the second inning and a two-run shot off him in the fourth.

He described his resiliency as similar to the team's.

"We're so loosey-goosey," Damon said. "After we were down, 3-0, we didn't panic. We were joking about packing up our things, kind of playing devil's advocate by thinking of the worst things possible and making sure the good things happened."

The Yankees, who were 0-12 in postseason series after losing three straight games, pulled out all the stops trying to reverse the futility, even enlisting Dent to toss a ceremonial first pitch in the rematch of last year's historic showdown. But Dent was no Ortiz, who smashed a two-run homer off Yankees starter Kevin Brown in the first inning. And he was no Bellhorn, who added a solo shot off Tom Gordon in the eighth.

The Sox built such a whopping lead that they hardly blinked when Pedro Martinez, making his first relief appearance since his memorable performance in Game 5 of the 1999 Division Series against the Indians, surrendered two runs on three hits in the seventh inning.

With the ownership troika of Henry, Lucchino, and Tom Werner watching the winner-take-all finale from a box next to the team's dugout, the Sox became the first team to beat the Yankees in the final two games of a best-of-seven series in the Bronx since the Cardinals in 1926. (The Sox opened the '26 season with a lineup led by center fielder Ira Flagstead, third baseman Fred Haney, right fielder Si Rosenthal, and first baseman Phil Todt). Heck, why not dedicate the victory to the '26 Sox as well? Every Sox team for a century has wanted a piece of the Yankees.

Long before the champagne corks popped last night in the visiting clubhouse in the bowels of The House That Ruth Built, the game appeared to take a bleak turn for the Sox within minutes of the first pitch. After Damon singled leading off the first inning and stole second, third base coach Dale Sveum waved him home on a single to left by Manny Ramirez, only for the Yankees to erase Damon on Jeter's relay from Hideki Matsui to Jorge Posada.

But no sooner did Damon dust himself off than Ortiz picked up Sveum by belting the next pitch from Brown (an 88-mile-per-hour fastball) into the right-field stands for a two-run shot, his third homer of the se-

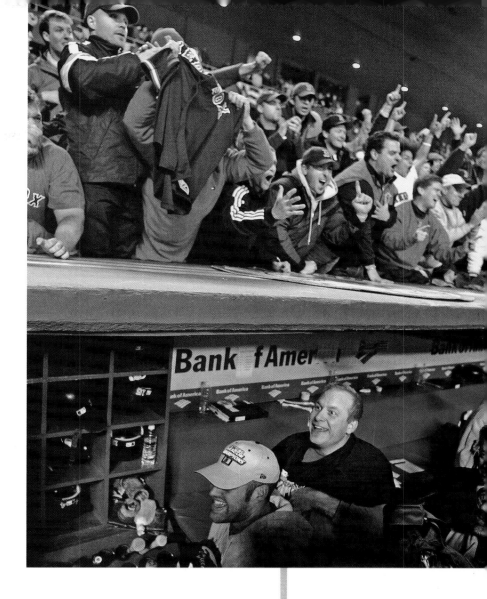

ries and fourth of the postseason. Lowe took the 2-0 lead and ran with it, retiring the Yankees in order quickly in the first to give the Sox another shot at Brown. And, boy, did they make the most of it.

Millar started a big rally for the second straight night, this time by lining a one-out single up the middle. Brown then did the Yankees no favors by issuing consecutive walks to Bill Mueller and Orlando Cabrera to load the bases for Damon, who was homerless in the postseason.

No longer. With Brown gone after his brief run of ineffectiveness, the Yankees summoned Vazquez, the former Expo the Sox had coveted in recent years. They liked Vazquez even more after Damon helped destroy the Empire by drilling Vazquez's first pitch into the right-field seats for the grand slam. ☻

THE PARTY WAS ON IN THE RED SOX DUGOUT FOR PLAYERS AND FANS ALIKE

MIRACLE WORKERS

AFTER A FRUSTRATING FINISH IN GAME 7 THE YEAR BEFORE, THE RED SOX HAD PLENTY TO CELEBRATE IN YANKEE STADIUM AFTER MAKING A HISTORIC COMEBACK

By BOB HOHLER

Good start

ANAHEIM Who would have thought a bunch of idiots (their term, not ours) could look so smart playing the national pastime? ◆ Forget "Baseball for Dummies." The Red Sox continued crafting a revolutionary version of the primer in their own wacky image.

"We are not the cowboys anymore," Johnny Damon, the team's chief yo-yo, declared. "We are just the idiots this year. We feel like we can win every game, we feel like we have to have fun, and I think that's why this team is liked by so many people out there."

Especially in Boston, which has long prided itself on embracing nonconformists.

But not in Anaheim, where the idiot act didn't fool anybody as the Sox played nearly every facet of the game as if they invented it in shellacking the Halos, 9-3, in Game 1 of the Division Series before 44,608 at Angel Stadium.

"If they are, they are idiots who can play ball," Anaheim manager Mike Scioscia said. "I tell you, they are tough."

	1	2	3	4	5	6	7	8	9		R	H	E
BOS	1	0	0	7	0	0	0	1	0		9	11	1
ANA	0	1	0	1	0	0	2	0	0		3	9	1

OCT. 6, 2004 • SCHILLING VS WASHBURN

JASON VARITEK
SCORES ON AN
ERROR BY CHONE
FIGGINS TO GET THE
SOX ROLLING

CURT SCHILLING WAS IN CONTROL FROM THE START BUT WOULD HURT HIS ANKLE LATER

Actually, Sox manager Terry Francona thought Damon calling his boys idiots might be a tad too harsh. Francona indicated his renegades may be the idiot savants of baseball.

"As a group, they are borderline nuts," he said. "But when they get out in the field, I think they try to play the game right."

Curt Schilling may just be crazy enough to believe he can all but singlehandedly fulfill the championship-famished franchise's unrequited dream. He took the first giant step toward the postseason promised land as he pinned the opening defeat on the Angels, surrendering three runs over 6 innings to improve his career playoff record to 6-1 with a 1.74 ERA (he has not lost in the postseason since 1993 with the Phillies).

"He's everything you saw," said Kevin Millar, who launched a two-run homer in a seven-run fourth inning, the biggest in postseason history for the Sox. "The guy's a horse. He's the most prepared pitcher out there. He's got great postseason experience, and he did everything we could ask of him. He went out there and gave us a chance to win."

Manny Ramirez, another madcap member of Damon's posse, also came up big, rocking a three-run homer and a first-inning double. Nutty as it may sound, Ramirez insisted he was just having fun.

"You only live one time," he said. "It's easy when you're happy and everything is going good. The days go so fast. When you're mad, they go forever."

The day flew for the Sox as they seized the advantage in the best-of-five series with Pedro Martinez prepared to start Game 2 against Bartolo Colon. It felt much sweeter to the Sox than the early days of last year's Division Series, when they dropped the first two games to the A's before they swept the final three to advance to the fateful second round against the Yankees.

"We came in and played the way we were supposed to play," Gabe Kapler said. "Schill pitched the way he was supposed to pitch and Manny swung the bat the way he's supposed to swing the bat. It takes contributions from everybody up and down the roster, but at the same time the big boys have to do their thing. They did it today."

The Sox also played smooth defense, save for an injury-related error by Schilling that helped the Angels score a consolation run as they trailed, 8-2, in the seventh inning. No one was smoother in the field than shortstop Orlando Cabrera, who showed no signs that he was affected by playing his first postseason game.

"Orlando is phenomenal, has been since the day he got here," Schilling said. "He is a game-changer in the field."

With the Sox leading, 1-0, in the third inning — thanks to Ramirez hustling his way to the double off Anaheim starter Jarrod Washburn and scoring on a single by his bashing buddy, David Ortiz — the Angels had runners at the corners with two outs when Cabrera submitted his first dandy play. He charged a slow roller by Garret Anderson and fired off-balance to nail Anderson and snuff the threat.

"I thought he hit it harder than he did," Cabrera said. "When I saw the ball almost dying in the grass, I tried to charge it real fast and get rid of it real quick because he's a pretty good runner. It was good because we got the momentum for the fourth inning."

The Sox seized it as Millar followed Or-tiz's leadoff walk by launching his second homer in as many postseason games (he homered in Game 7 of the AL Championship Series last year against the Yankees) for a 3-1 lead. Millar laid off an inside fastball before Washburn tried to fool him.

"He came back with a changeup," Millar said, "and I just got the barrel on the ball, thank God."

By the time Anaheim third baseman Chone Figgins made a two-run throwing error on Damon's grounder and Ramirez uncorked his homer, the Sox had all the runs they needed with an 8-1 lead.

"Millar's home run was definitely the biggest," Damon said. "But Manny's home run, that was the clincher."

Cabrera chipped in again in the sixth inning as he ranged to the right of second base to field a grounder by Bengie Molina and threw him out thanks in part to a nice scoop by Millar and Molina's slow feet.

"There was nothing special about that play," Cabrera said. "He's probably the only one I could throw out."

No matter. Cabrera's fellow former Gold Glover, Doug Mientkiewicz, tipped his hat to both Cabrera and Millar.

"Those plays to kill a rally are just as big as hitting a ball over the fence," he said.

Mientkiewicz, who replaced Millar in the seventh inning, helped seal the win by laying down a nifty RBI bunt single in the eighth. With two outs, he dropped it toward third base, allowing Damon to score easily from third.

"It's not about how fast you are, it's where you put it," Mientkiewicz said. "To me, that's a big run because they had the momentum coming back and we scored right there and turned it around."

As sweet as winning the opener was for the Sox, the Angels figured they have history on their side. They lost the opener of every postseason series in 2002 en route to a world championship.

"There's no cause for alarm," Washburn said. "Obviously, you'd like to win the first game, but we're not dead."

The Sox know that.

"It's great to be up, 1-0, but it's just one game," Damon said. "We're not going to be satisfied by just splitting. Now we need to try to win [Game 2] and let the cards fall where they may."

Damon added, in a stage whisper, "I think I might have the better cards." ☺

STATISTICS

Boston

BATTER	AB	R	H	BI	AVG.
Damon cf	5	2	2	0	.400
Bellhorn	4	0	0	0	.000
Reese	0	0	0	0	—
M. Ramirez	5	2	2	3	.400
D. Ortiz	3	1	1	1	.333
Millar	4	1	2	2	.500
Mientkiewicz	1	0	0	0	.000
Varitek	5	1	1	0	.200
Cabrera	3	1	1	0	.333
Mueller	4	0	0	0	.000
Kapler	5	1	1	0	.200

PITCHER	IP	H	R	ER	ERA
Schilling (W)	6.2	9	3	2	2.70
Embree	0.1	0	0	0	0.00
Timlin	2	0	0	0	0.00

Anaheim

BATTER	AB	R	H	BI	AVG.
Figgins	5	0	1	0	.200
Erstad	4	1	3	1	.750
Guerrero	5	0	0	0	.000
Anderson	4	1	0	0	.000
Glaus	3	1	3	2	1.000
DaVanon	3	0	0	0	.000
Riggs ph	1	0	0	0	.000
Molina	4	0	1	0	.250
Eckstein	4	0	1	0	.250
Amezaga	1	0	0	0	.000
McPherson	3	0	0	0	.000

PITCHER	IP	H	R	ER	ERA
Washburn (L)	3.1	5	7	3	8.10
Shields	1.2	1	1	1	5.40
Gregg	2	3	0	0	0.00
R. Ortiz	2	2	1	1	4.50

By BOB HOHLER

Second help

ANAHEIM Remember this about Johnny Damon dubbing his happy-go-lucky band of brothers a bunch of idiots. He never meant their baseball IQ bordered on brainless. Damon pictured his long-haired, corn-rowed, Harley-

riding Red Sox pals more like manager Terry Francona viewed them: "A bit unique in a lovable kind of way."

Sometimes they go astray. They may catnap on the basepaths, as Mark Bellhorn did in the second inning when he strayed off second base with the bases loaded and got thrown out in a lapse that snuffed a promising rally. And they may on occasion falter in the field, as Orlando Cabrera and Manny Ramirez did in the fifth when they muffed an easy pop to ignite an Anaheim rally.

But, for the love of Pete (in this case Pedro), they find their way home more often than not, as they did in stunning the Angels, 8-3, before 45,118 on Gene Autry Way to seize a 2-0 lead in the best-of-five Division Series and put Bronson Arroyo in position to help sweep the series.

"We feel great," Damon said. "Going back 2-0 with a day off today, you can't ask for much better than that."

MVP candidate Ramirez struck the decisive blow when he launched a sacrifice fly with one out in the seventh inning amid a 3-3 stalemate to drive in Damon.

The Sox waged the pivotal rally against Anaheim's bullpen dynamo, Francisco Rodriguez, who chipped in by wild-pitching Damon to third after Damon bounced into a fielder's choice and stole second.

Then the lovable ones broke the game open with four runs in the ninth, with Trot Nixon's RBI single and Cabrera's three-run double the big hits.

"We were down 0-2 last year, so we know how that is," Kevin Millar said. "We're going to go in there and try to give our best effort and try to get this thing over with."

As for Martinez, he made plenty of his own magic in the lovefest as he answered the doomsayers by working seven strong innings to lead the Sox to the threshold of their second straight berth in the American League Championship Series. Firing 116 pitches, one shy of his season high, and regularly hitting 94-96 miles per hour on the radar gun, Martinez rationed the Halos three runs on six hits, two walks, and a hit batsman for his first postseason win since he helped clinch the Division Series in Game 5 last year against the A's.

"A lot of people doubted the man," said

BOS	0 1 0	0 0 2	1 0 4	**8 12 0**
ANA	0 1 0	0 2 0	0 0 0	**3 7 0**

OCT. 7, 2004 • MARTINEZ VS COLON

Varitek, who launched a crucial, two-run homer in the sixth inning off Angels starter Bartolo Colon to erase a 3-1 deficit. "And I don't doubt that man."

Enough of the "trash-talking," Martinez said, about him being miffed that Curt Schilling got the Game 1 start rather than him. Martinez said he has a strong relationship with Schilling.

"To me, every time they give me the ball, I am number one," he said. "I don't believe what the experts say. I'm just here to do my job and I'll do it anywhere you put me."

"He's back," Millar said. "This guy shows you why he's one of the best going."

Ramirez also drove in the first Sox run by drawing a bases-loaded walk in the second inning.

While Martinez improved to 10-1 in 14 career starts against the Angels, the Sox

seized a 2-0 lead in a postseason series for only the fourth time in franchise history. They also did so en route to winning the 1916 World Series and 1975 ALCS, and on the way to losing the 1986 World Series.

This time, there was no way Martinez would return for the eighth. Everyone knew it, and when he departed after the seventh, he embraced nearly every teammate in the dugout.

Then he left it to the pen, which the Angels made battle for every out in the eighth. After Darin Erstad singled off Mike Timlin to open the inning, Timlin capped a seven-pitch struggle with Vladimir Guerrero by fanning the ever-dangerous slugger. Next came Mike Myers, who submarined Garret Anderson, catching him waving at a curveball for a third strike. And Keith Foulke followed, getting Troy Glaus looking on a borderline called third strike.

Foulke then mowed down the Angels in the ninth after the Sox all but put the game out of reach in the top of the inning. But Foulke knows the risks of a five-game series, even with a 2-0 lead. He and the Oakland A's lost an ALDS to the Sox last year after winning Games 1 and 2.

"It's definitely no walk in the park," Foulke said. "But these guys came in with a lot of momentum. Realistically, you just want to get one, so this is great."

Amid the 3-3 deadlock in the seventh, Bill Mueller helped break the logjam by narrowly beating out a grounder to second for a single. Damon's fielder's choice forced out Dave Roberts, who was running for Mueller, before Bellhorn contributed by drawing his second walk of the game. Up came Ramirez, who waved up the runners on Rodriguez's wild pitch before delivering his sacrifice fly.

If nothing else, Martinez wanted to prove his four-game losing streak — his longest ever in a single season — was a fluke. He had logged a 7.72 ERA during the slide, with his numbers deteriorating the deeper he pitched into the month and the less he rested between starts. Pitching on four days' rest in his last three winless starts of the season, he posted a 9.35 ERA, perhaps a sign of fatigue.

The fact was, Martinez, like co-ace Curt Schilling, fared considerably better pitching on five days' or more rest this season than on four. Martinez went 8-3 with a 3.16 ERA pitching with five or more days' of rest, 8-6 with a 4.53 ERA on four days.

So the Sox took heart that he was facing the Angels on six days' rest. And the early returns were promising. Unlike his previous two starts, when he fired his first pitches 88 m.p.h., Martinez opened at 92 and cranked it up to 96 as early as the second inning. His breaking ball and changeup looked sharp enough to nicely complement his fastball as he breezed through the first inning.

But the Sox offense had done him no favors in the top of the inning. After loading the bases with one out on a couple of flared singles by Damon and Bellhorn and a walk to David Ortiz, the Sox let the opportunity slip away when Nixon flied out to shallow left on the first pitch he saw from Colon and Millar grounded out on a 3-2 fastball.

The Sox fared only marginally better when they loaded the bases again in the second. This time, they did it with two outs on singles by Mueller and Damon and a walk to Bellhorn. But no sooner did Ramirez capitalize by drawing a walk on a 3-2 fastball from Colon to force in the game's first run (after just missing an opposite-field grand slam when his drive veered foul of the right-field pole) than Bellhorn blundered.

Boy, did he blunder. With Ortiz batting and the bases still loaded, Angels catcher Jose Molina snagged a 1-0 strike from Colon and fired a strike of his own to second base, catching Bellhorn leaning toward third in no-man's land. Bellhorn slipped a bit as he scrambled to get back to second, but he arrived way too late as David Eckstein applied the tag.

The Angels seemed to seize some momentum from Boston's early woes. Martinez contributed to the cause by walking Glaus leading off the bottom of the second. At that, Jeff DaVanon grounded a 96-m.p.h. fastball to left for a single, sending Glaus to second, and rookie Dallas McPherson, facing Martinez for the first time, poked an opposite-field single to left, allowing Glaus to dash home for a 1-1 tie.

Martinez encounterd more trouble in the fifth. First, Molina (0 for 5 in his career against Martinez) lifted a pop to shallow left center. Cabrera ranged back from short as if he were going to grab it, prompting Ramirez, who also seemingly could have caught the ball, to slow down. But then Cabrera suddenly cut off his pursuit, allowing the ball to drop for a leadoff single.

Martinez aggravated matters by letting the next batter, Eckstein, rifle an 0-2 curveball to center, moving Molina to second. A batter later, Martinez drilled Erstad on the left knee with a cut fastball, loading the bases with one out for Guerrero. And Guerrero quickly made him pay by lacing a misplaced, 94-m.p.h. heater to right-center for a two-run single, staking Colon to a 3-1 lead.

Meanwhile, Colon retired nine straight batters after Bellhorn's gaffe. Ortiz ended the streak by hustling out a grounder to short for a leadoff single in the sixth. Ortiz's hit went for naught as Nixon bounced into a double play. But after Millar kept the inning alive by sneaking a grounder up the middle past the diving Eckstein for a single, Varitek walloped the next pitch into the right-field stands to pull the Sox even, 3-3. ☺

STATISTICS

Boston

BATTER	AB	R	H	BI	AVG.
Damon	5	1	2	0	.400
Bellhorn	3	0	1	0	.143
Reese	0	0	0	0	000
Ramirez	3	1	1	2	.375
Ortiz	2	1	1	0	.400
Nixon	5	0	1	1	.200
Kapler pr	0	1	0	0	200
Millar	3	1	1	0	.429
Mientkiewicz	2	0	1	0	.667
Varitek	3	2	1	2	.250
Cabrera	5	0	1	3	.250
Mueller	3	1	2	0	.286
Roberts	0	0	0	0	000
Youkilis	2	0	0	0	.000

PITCHER	IP	H	R	ER	ERA
Martinez (W)	7	6	3	3	3.86
Timlin	0.1	1	0	0	0.00
Myers	0.1	0	0	0	0.00
Foulke (S)	1.1	0	0	0	0.00

Anaheim

BATTER	AB	R	H	BI	AVG.
Figgins	4	0	0	0	.111
Erstad	3	0	1	0	.571
Guerrero	3	0	1	2	.125
Anderson	4	0	0	0	.000
Glaus	3	1	0	0	.500
DaVanon	4	0	2	0	.286
Mcpherson	4	0	1	1	.143
J. Molina	2	1	1	0	.500
Kotchman ph	1	0	0	0	.000
B. Molina	0	0	0	0	250
Pride ph	1	0	0	0	.000
Eckstein	3	1	1	0	.286

PITCHER	IP	H	R	ER	ERA
Colon	6	7	3	3	4.50
Rodriguez (L)	2	2	1	1	4.50
Donnelly	1	3	4	4	36.0

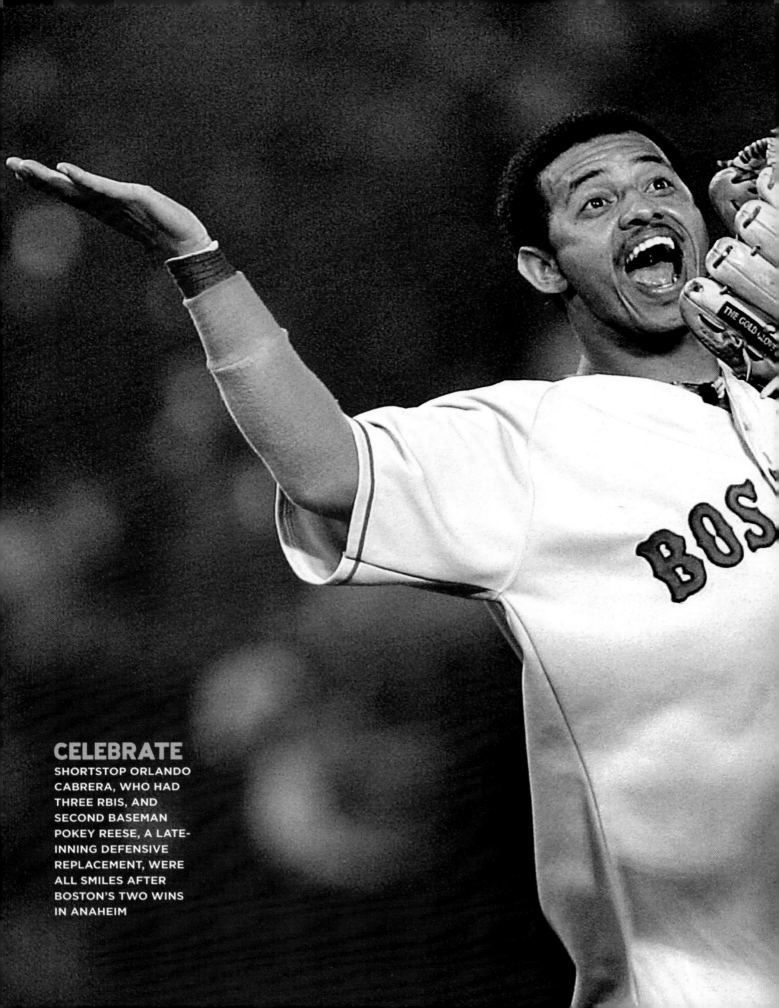

CELEBRATE

SHORTSTOP ORLANDO
CABRERA, WHO HAD
THREE RBIS, AND
SECOND BASEMAN
POKEY REESE, A LATE-
INNING DEFENSIVE
REPLACEMENT, WERE
ALL SMILES AFTER
BOSTON'S TWO WINS
IN ANAHEIM

By BOB HOHLER

David, goliath

BOSTON Poor David Ortiz. All he had to protect him were his silly little goggles as his teammates ambushed him in the postgame frenzy.

A bottle of Great Western here, a bucket of water there, everywhere liquid splashing over him as one teammate after another — from a minimum-salaried rookie to his $160-million pal, Manny Ramirez — paid voracious tribute to the smiling slugger.

And why not? In a blast that may be remembered by the first generation of New Englanders in the 21st century as famously as a previous generation recalls Carlton Fisk's momentous shot in Game 6 of the '75 World Series, Ortiz further emblazoned his image in franchise history by torquing a misplaced slider from Jarrod Washburn over the Monster with two outs in the 10th inning for a two-run shot that catapulted the Sox to an electrifying 8-6 victory over the Angels and a sweep of the best-of-five Division Series.

Splish, splash. Next stop the American League Championship Series against the

ANA	0 0 0	1 0 0	5 0 0	0	6 8 2
BOS	0 0 2	3 1 0	0 0 0	2	8 12 0

OCT. 9, 2004 • ARROYO VS ESCOBAR

IT WAS HATS OFF
TO DAVID ORTIZ
AFTER HIS
TWO-RUN HOMER
IN THE TENTH
TO WIN

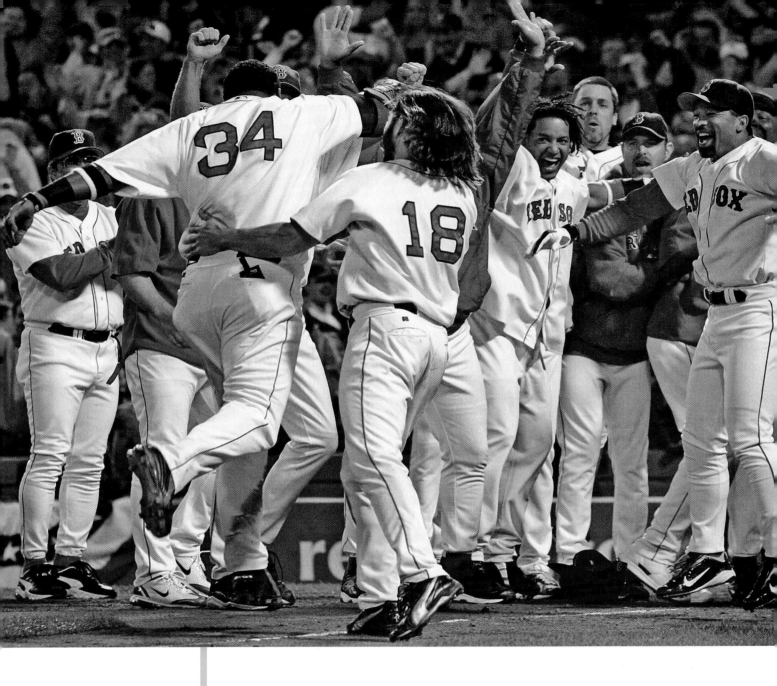

Yankees or Twins.

"It was a classic from start to finish and a real fitting way for us to get through the first round," general manager Theo Epstein said amid the sudsy celebration in the Sox clubhouse. "It's pretty sweet. Now we have two more celebrations to go."

Ortiz almost seemed to take it in stride amid the postgame mayhem. Johnny Damon set the stage for the winning shot by singling to lead off the 10th against Francisco Rodriguez.

"I was looking for a pitch I could drive and I got it," Ortiz said, so drenched in suds he could hardly speak. "He threw me a slider he left a little bit high, and here we are."

Simple enough — until you realize how narrowly they escaped one of the most mortifying postseason losses since, well, last October. After blowing a 6-1 lead in the seventh inning, the Sox flashed their signature resilience to ice their second consecutive trip to the ALCS for the first time since the format began in 1969. The sweep was only their second in 20 postseason series since 1903.

"I was begging," manager Terry Francona said of watching Ortiz's drive soar through the night with 35,547 others in the park begging with him. "There was a lot of begging going on."

The victory allowed the Sox to celebrate

clinching their first playoff series at Fenway Park since the 1986 league championship series. But to stage their latest feat, they needed to overcome blowing the largest lead (five runs) by a home team in postseason history.

As Epstein has said often before, "We don't do anything easy."

The worm turned on them this time after Bronson Arroyo departed leading, 6-1, with none out and a runner on first in the seventh after a sensational start. On came Mike Myers, who did the Sox no favors by walking the only batter he faced, pinch hitter Jose Molina, to put runners at first and second. Then came Mike Timlin, who promptly retired Curtis Pride for the first out before David Eckstein flared an opposite-field single to right, loading the bases.

Timlin responded by throwing three straight strikes past Chone Figgins. Then he got ahead in the count, 0-and-2, against Darin Erstad before he ultimately lost a seven-pitch showdown to force in a run, making it 6-2.

Still, the champagne chilled. But after Timlin fired a 91-mile-per-hour fastball for a strike on his first pitch to Vladimir Guerrero, he tried to improve his position by coming back with a 92-m.p.h. heater over the heart of the plate.

Bad choice. Guerrero got a bead on it and blasted it into the Sox pen for the tying slam.

"I threw a bad pitch to a really good hitter," Timlin said. "I had beaten him a couple of times and it was his turn to beat me. That's why they have averages."

The devastating shot spoiled a memorable outing by Arroyo, who had surrendered only two runs on three hits and a pair of walks until he handed off to the pen.

"When they came back like that, we kind of were like, 'Oh [expletive],'" Damon said. "That team is a pain in the butt, but we couldn't let them win this game. If they won, the momentum would have shifted. We would have to wake up early and play again, and we're not morning people."

So they went to work, with Alan Embree getting the Sox out of the seventh before he handed off to Keith Foulke with one out in the eighth. Foulke walked a tightrope, tiptoeing out of a bases-loaded jam in the ninth before he passed the torch to Derek Lowe, who escaped a mess with runners at first and third in the 10th.

"We had so many different chances to lose that game," Epstein said, "but we showed huge heart time and time again."

Timlin credited the team's dauntless spirit.

"We have guys who don't quit and don't want to lose," he said. ⚾

STATISTICS

Anaheim

BATTER	AB	R	H	BI	AVG.
Figgins	5	0	1	0	.143
Erstad	3	1	1	1	.500
Guerrero	4	1	1	4	.167
Anderson	5	0	2	0	.154
Glaus	5	1	1	1	.364
DaVanon	3	1	0	0	.200
B. Molina	2	0	0	0	.167
Kotchman ph	0	0	0	0	.000
J. Molina ph	1	1	0	0	.333
Mcpherson	2	0	0	0	.111
Riggs ph	0	0	0	0	.000
Pride ph	1	0	0	0	.000
Amezaga	1	0	0	0	.000
Eckstein	5	1	2	0	.333

PITCHER	IP	H	R	ER	ERA
Escobar	3.1	5	5	3	8.10
Shields	1.1	4	1	1	6.00
Donnelly	2.1	0	0	0	10.80
Rodriguez (L)	2.2	2	1	1	3.86
Washburn	0	1	1	1	10.80

Boston

BATTER	AB	R	H	BI	AVG.
Damon	5	1	3	0	.467
Bellhorn	4	2	0	0	.091
Reese pr	0	1	0	0	—
Ramirez	5	0	2	22	.385
D. Ortiz	6	2	4	3	.545
Nixon	3	0	1	1	.250
Millar	3	0	0	2	.300
Mientkiewicz	1	0	0	0	.500
Varitek	4	0	0	0	.167
Cabrera	5	0	0	0	.154
Mueller	5	2	2	0	.333

PITCHER	IP	H	R	ER	ERA
Arroyo	6	3	2	2	3.00
Myers	0	0	1	1	27.00
Timlin	0.2	2	3	3	9.00
Embree	0.2	0	0	0	0.00
Foulke	1.2	2	0	0	0.00
Lowe (W)	1	1	0	0	0.00

BRONSON ARROYO GAVE THE SOX A STAND-UP PERFORMANCE IN SIX INNINGS AS THE STARTER

By DAN SHAUGNESSY

The recap

The last two Saturdays of July changed the 2004 Boston baseball season. Before the final two weekends of the seventh month, the Red Sox were alarmingly average. The Olde Towne Team, swollen with the second-highest

payroll ($130 million) in the majors, was finishing a third consecutive month of .500 baseball and a season of great expectations looked like it might go down as the most disappointing campaign in the storied history of the franchise.

And then two things happened, one on the field and one in the executive offices of 4 Yawkey Way. On July 24, after a near-washout because of torrential morning rains, the Red Sox players demanded to take the field for a nationally televised game against the hated Yankees. Just when it looked like they were going to get picked on by the New York bullies once again, Boston catcher Jason Varitek woke up a moribund ball club and a Nation by stuffing his mitt into the loud mouth of one Alex Rodriguez - the very same A-Rod who had been the dominant figure of the Hub hardball nuclear winter of 2003-04.

A week later, while the Sox were in the visitor's clubhouse of the Metrodome in Minneapolis, 30-year-old general manag-

er Theo Epstein pulled the trigger on the most sensational Red Sox player transaction since Babe Ruth was sold to the Yankees in 1920. Convinced that his team could not win the World Series as constituted, wary that Nomar Garciaparra's nagging injury was going to drag down the team, and certain that the star shortstop was going to walk at the end of the season, Epstein traded Garciaparra to the Chicago Cubs.

The impact of the deal was felt immediately in Boston souvenir stores, where No. 5 jerseys flew off the racks, and in New England households, where young children cried themselves to sleep. But then an odd thing happened: the Red Sox started playing better. They took better care of the baseball, no longer leading the majors in unearned runs allowed. They started winning one-run games. They started hitting in the clutch. No longer worried about getting 30 outs per game, pitchers suddenly had more confidence. Manager Terry Francona got smarter.

When they started to win, the sprit of 2003 returned. New handshakes were invented. The Red Sox were the Pointer Brothers, kings of congratulations. Manny Ramirez and David Ortiz continued their assault on the 40-homer plateau and possible MVP honors. Kevin Millar started to slug. New shortstop Orlando Cabrera caught everything in sight and most important, played every day. Curt Schilling won just about every time he set foot on the mound and Pedro Martinez made every start. And Johnny Damon let his hair grow down past his shoulders, standing in center field as the symbol of the born-to-be-wild Red Sox.

They went 21-7 in August and won 20 of 22 games in a memorable stretch of August and September, pulling to within two games of the first-place Yankees after trailing by 10 1/2 on the morning of Aug. 16. The streak, which included an 8-1 dusting of the Angels, Rangers, and A's, gave them a firm grip on the American League wild-card playoff spot, which they clinched one week ago today with a champagne-soaked victory at the Tropicana Dome in St. Petersburg, Fla.

So now the Red Sox are in the postseason for the 11th time since last winning a World Series in 1918. They open tomorrow against the Angels in the first game of a best-of-five. Following the philosophy of John Fitzgerald Kennedy, most

JASON VARITEK'S IN-YOUR-FACE MOVE AGAINST ALEX RODRIGUEZ ON JULY 24 BROUGHT THE RED SOX ALIVE FOR THE LAST TWO MONTHS OF THE SEASON

Sox fans are skeptical idealists on the eve of baseball's Octoberfest.

Here's how they arrived at this critical moment in franchise history:

The Fall

There is no way to examine this season without beginning at the end of 2003. The Sox were five outs from the World Series on the night of Oct. 16, when a tired Martinez was left on the mound to cough up the game against the Yankees. Grady Little almost became the first manager to be fired in the middle of a playoff game. When Aaron Boone's walkoff homer dropped into left field stands at 12:16 a.m., Little's fate was sealed. He was officially dismissed two days after the World Series ended and the Sox commenced a managerial search that produced Francona. When Francona, a four-year loser in Philadelphia, was hired, some wondered, "Is the guy too nice?" The fear proved to be legitimate.

The Winter

Never has a Boston baseball team been a bigger newsmaker during an offseason. It proved embarrassing to Epstein and his staff. At one point, Young Theo implored the New England media to turn its sights on the local football team, which was experiencing a fair amount of success. Didn't matter. The Sox dominated the headlines. Two days after the manager was fired, Ramirez was put on irrevocable waivers, but no team claimed him. Still, the message was loud and clear. Epstein went to Arizona for Thanksgiving dinner with the Schillings and came away with a pitcher who would win 21 games. After agreeing to a contract (waiving a no-trade clause), Schilling made the first of one million Curt commentaries, announcing, "I guess I hate the Yankees now." The Sox also signed Oakland closer Keith Foulke.

But it was the A-Rod negotiations that dominated the hot stove during the cold months. Sox owner John W. Henry received permission to court the Texas MVP shortstop and the ultimate bombshell dropped when the Sox, Rangers, and White Sox agreed on deals that would have landed Manny in Texas, A-Rod in Boston, Nomar in Chicago, and slugging White Sox outfielder Magglio Ordonez

in Boston. Alas, union chief Gene Orza blocked the deal, and before you could say "George Costanza" the Yankees swooped in, got A-Rod to agree to play third, and completed a trade that landed the quarter-billion-dollar man in the Bronx. The Red Sox looked ridiculous and Henry compounded the folly by complaining about the Yankees' deep pockets. To stop the name-calling, commissioner Bud Selig had to put a gag order on the front offices. Who would have guessed that in 2004, Ramirez would be a more valuable asset than Rodriguez?

The Spring

Epstein, along with seven or eight young co-workers, moved into a large house in Cape Coral, Fla., at the beginning of spring training. Sox clubhouse attendant Tommy McLaughlin dubbed it "Phi Sign-a Player." The GM was under great scrutiny because Garciaparra, Martinez, Derek Lowe, Varitek, and David Ortiz were all entering the final years of their contracts. It was a dominant issue throughout spring training. Ortiz eventually signed and Garciaparra was traded, but the other three are potential free agents as the Red Sox wade into playoff waters.

Damon set the tone for the Delta House Red Sox when he arrived in Florida looking like a cross between Charles Manson and Jesus Christ. Epstein immediately told Damon it was OK to keep the long hair and beard, establishing the Sox locker room as the Hair Club For Men throughout 2004. The theme was, if it feels good, do it. If anything went wrong, it was left for the suddenly happy Ramirez to tell everyone to "turn the page."

Other than a couple of over-hyped exhibitions with the Yankees (spring training seats fetching $500?), the big news out of Fort Myers was Garciaparra's mysterious Achilles' injury. Citing an alleged batting practice incident when a ball hit off his heel, which nobody saw, Garciaparra sat down and didn't come back until early June. He went 0 for 8 in Florida and did not play an inning after St. Patrick's Day. Francona kept saying he expected Garciaparra to be ready for Opening Day, almost right up until the opener in Baltimore. The other bad news in Florida was Trot Nixon's back pain, which also put him on the shelf to start the season.

The Sox lost the opener on a frigid night in Baltimore and Pedro made news by leaving the ballpark before the game was over. Francona promptly took the blame for his ace, saying he hadn't explained the rules properly. That would be a theme throughout 2004; no matter what his players did, the manager would say, "I love these guys," and take the blame.

Making A-Rod and Jeter look like bums, the Sox won six of seven against the Yankees in April and finished the month with a record of 15-6. On the first of May in Texas, Martinez complained about his contract status and accused Sox management of lying. The remarks were followed by a five-game losing streak and three months of .500 ball.

In the miserable months of May and June, and most of July, the Sox floundered because of poor defense, lack of timely hitting, and disappointing performances from some starters, particularly Lowe. They seemed to lose all the close games. Garciaparra didn't come back until June 9, and then he was a part-time player who could no longer make routine plays in the field. Nixon added a quadriceps injury to his back woes and seemed to be lost for the season. Batting champ Bill Mueller required knee surgery and went on the shelf in late May.

The Summer

On the first day of July, the Sox and Yankees engaged in an epic 13-inning bout at Yankee Stadium. The Yankees won it, 5-4, with a two-out rally in the bottom of the 13th, but the lasting memory is of Jeter diving into the stands to catch a popup in the 12th while Garciaparra sat and watched the entire game from the Sox bench.

While Garciaparra pouted and missed balls when he did play, Ramirez was a new man. He joked with fans, teammates, even reporters. He enjoyed every moment. And he crushed every baseball. Ramirez joined Ortiz, Schilling, Damon, and Martinez as fan favorites.

The Sox still were giving away runs and games in early July when Epstein made the decision to trade Garciaparra. The game in New York was a loud statement that something had to be done. On the day Varitek challenged A-Rod, in the most dramatic game of the season, the Sox beat the Yankees, 11-10, on Mueller's walkoff homer off Mariano Rivera. The next night, while Presidential nominee-to-be John Kerry watched from Henrytown on the eve of the Democratic National Convention, the Sox beat the Yankees again, 9-6, then hit the road for Balti-

NOMAR GARCIAPRRA, LIKE JOHNNY PESKY, WAS SYNONYMOUS WITH THE RED SOX UNTIL HE WAS TRADED TO CHICAGO

more, Minnesota, and Tampa. Garciaparra popped to Jeter in his final Red Sox at-bat at Fenway Park. While the team was in Baltimore, Garciaparra told the training staff and Francona that he was going to need more time off, maybe even have to go back to the disabled list. Already bothered by Garciaparra's inability to play average defense, the uncertainty of the situation forced Epstein to pursue a trade. The deal was struck in the final hours before the deadline and Garciaparra became a Cub while Cabrera and Doug Mientkiewicz joined the Red Sox, bolstering the team's infield defense.

The Red Sox lost the first two games after the trade, then went on a tear that has yet to subside. Ramirez and Ortiz became only the second Sox teammates (joining Carl Yastrzemski and Rico Petrocelli) to hit 40 homers in the same season. Millar became the hitter he was in the first half of 2003. Mueller came back and beefed up the bottom of the order. Damon hit over .300, reached 20 homers and put his name on some MVP ballots. Schilling won every start. Martinez made every start. Helped by the new infield defense, Lowe started to win regularly. All five Sox starters stayed healthy the entire season.

Cabrera stabilized the entire team. He made all the plays, contributed offensively, and gave his pitchers new confidence. Francona went to his bench and got help from Dave Roberts, Gabe Kapler, and Doug Mirabelli. Mark Bellhorn drove everyone crazy with his walks and strikeouts, but he was a surprisingly effective offensive weapon. There was skepticism when the "new" Red Sox beat up the likes of the Blue Jays, White Sox, and Tigers, but then they swept Anaheim at Fenway and the A's in Oakland and spawned a Nation of believers. Varitek said he thought the Red Sox were the best team in the AL.

As always, there was more business with the Yankees. New York never had blown a first-place lead of more than six games. The Sox cut it to two Sept. 8 and to 2½ when they rallied to beat Rivera again Friday night, Sept. 17, at Yankee Stadium (with the key hits by Cabrera and Damon). However, the Yankees routed Lowe Saturday afternoon, scored eight runs off Martinez in another rout Sunday, and went into cruise control to win another AL East title. When New York beat Martinez yet again ("The Yankees are my daddy," said the ace) Sept. 24, the Yankees led by 5½ games.

The Sox routed the Yankees in the fi-nal two Fenway showdowns, 12-5 and 11-4, finishing the year with an 11-8 re-cord against the Bombers. They clinched in Tampa Bay and spent the next six days being eliminated by the Yankees and try-ing to figure out whether they'd be flying to Minneapolis, Oakland, or Anaheim last night. At the end of the season, the greatest concern was a slumping Martinez, who lost his final four starts and, it seemed, much of his confidence. Meanwhile, Lowe struggled badly at the end of September and lost his spot in the postseason rotation.

In the end, they finished second to New York for a record seventh straight season, but they also won 98 games, more than any Boston team since 1978, when the Red Sox tied New York for first place before running into Bucky Dent. The 2004 Sox won more games than any of the last three Red Sox World Series qualifiers. But none of it will mean anything unless they win the World Series for the first time since 1918. ☻

THE SUN SHONE ON FENWAY AND THE SOX FROM THE VERY START

2004 REGULAR SEASON

DATE	OPPONENT	SCORE	PLACE	GAMES BEHIND		THE SKINNY
4/4	at Baltimore	L 7-2	t-5th	-1		Pedro Martinez loses season opener (again)
4/6	at Baltimore	W 4-1	t-2nd	-.5		Curt Schilling and Keith Foulke start off right
4/7	at Baltimore	10-3	1st		+.5	Offense shows its stuff: 10 runs on 14 hits
4/8	at Baltimore	3-2	t-2nd	-.5		Bobby Jones walks in winning run in 13th inning
4/9	Toronto	10-5	t-3rd	-1		Bullpen woes: 6 runs in 2 innings
4/10	Toronto	4-1	t-1st	0		David Ortiz and Manny Ramirez homer
4/11	Toronto	6-4	t-1st	0		Walk-off winner for Ortiz in 12th
4/15	Baltimore	12-7	t-2nd	-.5		Defense falters in 11th
4/16	NY Yankees	6-2	t-1st	0		Show of force: 3 homers
4/17	NY Yankees	5-2	t-1st	0		Schilling dominates for second win
4/18	NY Yankees	7-3	2nd	-1		Bombers rough up Derek Lowe early
4/19	NY Yankees	5-4	2nd	-.5		A Patriot Day rally for Sox
4/20	at Toronto	4-2	2nd	-.5		Martinez bests Roy Halladay again
4/21	at Toronto	4-2	1st		+.5	Doug Mirabelli goes deep twice
4/22	at Toronto	7-3	2nd	-.5		Jays get to Schilling late
4/23	at NY Yankees	11-2	2nd	-.5		Jose Contreras no match for Sox
4/24	at NY Yankees	3-2	1st		+.5	Bullpen shuts out Yankees for six innings
4/25	at NY Yankees	2-0	1st		+1.5	Pedro completes the sweep
4/28	Tampa Bay	6-0	1st		+2	Six runs more than enough for Schilling.
4/29	Tampa Bay	4-0	1st		+2	Third straight shutout for Sox pitching
4/29	Tampa Bay	7-3	1st		+2.5	Over quickly: 7 runs in 1st
MAY						
5/1	at Texas	4-3	1st		+2.5	Bullpen's scoreless streak ends at 32 innings
5/1	at Texas	8-5	1st		+2.5	A double loss: Pedro beaten
5/2	at Texas	4-1	1st		+1.5	R.A. Dickey leads Rangers sweep
5/3	at Cleveland	2-1	1st		+1	Jake Westbrook and Indians edge Schilling.
5/4	at Cleveland	7-6	t-1st	0		Sox lose 5th straight
5/5	at Cleveland	9-5	t-1st	0		Ortiz stops skid with 2 homers
5/6	at Cleveland	5-2	1st		+1	Pedro keeps it going
5/7	Kansas City	7-6	1st		+2	Rally Sox: Mark Bellhorn and Jason Varitek
5/8	Kansas City	9-1	1st		+2	Schilling goes 9, Sox score 9. No contest.
5/9	Kansas City	8-4	1st		+1	Lowe takes the loss
5/10	Cleveland	10-6	1st		+.5	Indians shake rattle and roll with 10 hits
5/11	Cleveland	5-3	1st		+.5	Three runs in 8th lift Sox
5/12	Cleveland	6-4	1st		+.5	Three more errors for the Sox defense
5/13	at Toronto	12-6	2nd	-.5		Jays get 9 runs in final 3 innings
5/14	at Toronto	9-3	2nd	-.5		Payback: Sox get 6 runs in the 8th
5/15	at Toronto	4-0	1st		+.5	Bronson Arroyo: 8 shutout innings
5/16	at Toronto	3-1	2nd	-.5		Halladay's turn to beat Pedro
5/18	at Tampa Bay	7-3	1st		+.5	Tim Wakefield wins one for his new son, Trevor.
5/19	at Tampa Bay	4-1	1st		+.5	Ramirez homer leads Sox past Rays.
5/20	at Tampa Bay	9-6	2nd	-.5		Lowe can't get out of 3rd, tagged for 7 runs.
5/21	Toronto	11-5	1st		+.5	Ramirez breaks tie in 8th
5/22	Toronto	5-2	1st		+1.5	Manny gets it started again
5/23	Toronto	7-2	1st		+1.5	Wakefield scatters 7 singles
5/25	Oakland	12-2	1st		+1.5	Sox get 19 hits off Tim Hudson
5/26	Oakland	9-6	1st		+1.5	A's give Sox a gift
5/27	Oakland	15-2	1st		+.5	A's get 15 runs on 19 hits

DATE	OPPONENT	SCORE	PLACE	GAMES BEHIND	THE SKINNY
5/28	Seattle	W 8-4	1st	+.5	Ramirez and Ortiz go deep
5/29	Seattle	L 5-4	2nd	-.5	Another Manny homer isn't enough
5/30	Seattle	9-7	1st	+.5	David McCarty homers in 12th
5/31	Baltimore	13-4	t-1st	0	Another Lowe point: 7 runs alowed

JUNE

DATE	OPPONENT	SCORE	PLACE	GAMES BEHIND	THE SKINNY
6/1	at Anaheim	7-6	2nd	-1	Vlad Guerrero doubles in 6th
6/2	at Anaheim	10-7	2nd	-2	The bullpen blows it
6/4	at Kansas City	5-2	2nd	-3.5	Jimmy Gobble retires 15 straight.
6/5	at Kansas City	8-4	2nd	-2.5	Sox snap skid, Schilling wins 7th.
6/6	at Kansas City	5-3	2nd	-2.5	Sox get five in sixth to rally.
6/8	San Diego	1-0	2nd	-2.5	Martinez kicks off inter-league play
6/9	San Diego	8-1	2nd	-3.5	Nomar Garciappara returns, 1-for-2
6/10	San Diego	9-3	2nd	-3.5	Nomar's 2-run double sparks Sox, Schilling
6/11	Los Angeles	2-1	2nd	-2.5	Ortiz bails out Foulke in the 9th
6/12	Los Angeles	14-5	2nd	-3.5	Wakefield gets hit hard
6/13	Los Angeles	4-1	2nd	-3.5	Glove story: Pokey Reese comes through
6/15	at Colorado	6-3	2nd	-4.5	Todd Helton and Vinny Castilla lead Rockies
6/16	at Colorado	7-6	2nd	-5.5	Late rally not enough
6/17	at Colorado	11-0	2nd	-4.5	Ortiz and Nomar: 3 hits each
6/18	at San Fran	14-9	2nd	-3.5	Long ball: 4 homers edge Giants.
6/19	at San Fran	6-4	2nd	-4.5	Edgardo Alfonso's 2-run HR beats Sox in 8th
6/20	at San Fran	4-0	2nd	-4.5	Sox get only one hit off Jason Schmidt
6/22	Minnesota	9-2	2nd	-4.5	Nomar's grand slam lifts Boston
6/23	Minnesota	4-2	2nd	-4.5	Tori Hunter homers
6/24	Minnesota	4-3	2nd	-5.5	Twins beat Foulke in 10th
6/25	Philadelphia	12-1	2nd	-5	Sox put up 8 runs in 6th
6/26	Philadelphia	9-2	2nd	-5	Jim Thome's 25th homer drops Sox
6/27	Philadelphia	12-3	2nd	-5.5	Tenth win for Schilling
6/29	at NY Yankees	11-3	2nd	-6.5	Yanks take advantage of Lowe and 3 errors
6/30	at NY Yankees	4-2	2nd	-7.5	Bombers get 2 in 7th and 2 in 8th for win

JULY

DATE	OPPONENT	SCORE	PLACE	GAMES BEHIND	THE SKINNY
7/1	at NY Yankees	5-4	2nd	-8.5	Derek Jeter goes into stands as Yanks sweep
7/2	at Atlanta	6-3	2nd	-8.5	Nick Green's 3-run homer in the 13th wins it
7/3	at Atlanta	6-1	2nd	-7.5	Schilling K's 10 in complete game.
7/4	at Atlanta	10-4	2nd	-7.5	Lowe suffers 5th inning meltdown
7/6	Oakland	11-0	2nd	-7	Johnny Damon singles 5 times
7/7	Oakland	11-3	2nd	-6	Ramirez, Garciaparra and Mark Bellhorn homer
7/8	Oakland	8-7	2nd	-6	Bill Mueller's 10th inning double gets series sweep
7/9	Texas	7-0	2nd	-6	Arroyo pitches 8 shutout innings
7/10	Texas	14-6	2nd	-6	Bat men: 14 runs, 21 hits, 4 homers
7/11	Texas	6-5	2nd	-7	Foulke gets tagged with a loss
7/15	at Anaheim	8-1	2nd	-8	Lowe gives up 5 in the 5th
7/16	at Anaheim	4-2	2nd	-7	Nomar homers and Pedro wins 6th straight
7/17	at Anaheim	8-3	2nd	-8	Vlad Guerrero strikes again with homer
7/18	at Anaheim	6-2	2nd	-7	Ortiz triples and homers for Schilling
7/19	at Seattle	8-4	2nd	-7	Brett Boone's 11th- inning grand slam sinks Sox
7/20	at Seattle	9-7	2nd	-7	An 8-run 4th inning gets Lowe his 8th win
7/21	Baltimore	10-5	2nd	-8	Orioles touch up Pedro for 8 runs
7/22	Baltimore	8-3	2nd	-8.5	O's top Sox in Abe Alvarez's major league debut

DATE	OPPONENT	SCORE	PLACE	GAMES BEHIND	THE SKINNY
7/22	Baltimore	W 4-0	2nd	-8.5	Despite 10 hits, O's can't score
7/23	NY Yankees	L 8-7	2nd	-9.5	A-Rod's 9th inning single wins it
7/24	NY Yankees,	11-10	2nd	-8.5	A fight and a win on Bill Mueller's walk-off homer
7/25	NY Yankees	9-6	2nd	-7.5	Contreras tagged for 8 runs
7/26	Baltimore	12-5	2nd	-7.5	Pedro gets early support
7/28	Baltimore	4-1	2nd	-8	Javy Lopez homers twice to beat Schilling.
7/30	at Minnesota	8-2	2nd	-7.5	Each Red Sox starter reaches base
7/31	at Minnesota	5-4	2nd	-8.5	Nomar is traded in four-team deal

AUGUST

DATE	OPPONENT	SCORE	PLACE	GAMES BEHIND	THE SKINNY
8/1	at Minnesota	4-3	2nd	-9.5	Twins score on sac fly and error in 8th inning
8/2	at Tampa Bay	6-3	2nd	-9	David McCarty's 3-run homer lifts the Sox
8/3	at Tampa Bay	5-2	2nd	-8	Schilling gets 3d complete game of the season.
8/4	at Tampa Bay	5-4	2nd	-9	Toby Hall's 7th-inning grand slam wins it
8/6	at Detroit	4-3	2nd	-10.5	Sox fall 10 behind the Yankees in AL East
8/7	at Detroit	7-4	2nd	-10.5	Pedro gets 69th double-digit strikeout game
8/8	at Detroit	11-9	2nd	-10.5	Sox outslug Tigers to give Wakefield win
8/9	Tampa Bay	8-3	2nd	-10.5	Schilling drops first decision at Fenway
8/10	Tampa Bay	8-4	2nd	-9.5	Bottom of the order drives in all 8 runs
8/11	Tampa Bay	14-4	2nd	-9.5	Kevin Millar: 4 hits, 4 RBIs in 5 innings
8/12	Tampa Bay	6-0	2nd	-9.5	Pedro gets 1st shutout in almost 4 years.
8/13	Chicago WS	8-7	2nd	-10.5	Contreras finally beats the Sox
8/14	Chicago WS	4-3	2nd	-10.5	Ortiz breaks 8th-inning tie with his 2d homer
8/15	Chicago WS	5-4	2nd	-10.5	Boston loads bases but can't get tying run
8/16	Toronto	8-4	2nd	-10	Doug Mientkiewicz makes first career start at 2b
8/17	Toronto	5-4	2nd	-9	Orlando Cabrera gets walk-off double
8/18	Toronto	6-4	2nd	-8	Sox a season-high 15 games over .500.
8/20	at Chicago WS	10-1	2nd	-7.5	Sox score 6 in the first 2 innings for Schilling
8/21	at Chicago WS	10-7	2nd	-6.5	Manny homers and gets 5 RBIs.
8/22	at Chicago WS	6-5	2nd	-5.5	Manny and Ortiz hit back-to-back HRs in 8th
8/23	at Toronto	3-0	2nd	-6.5	Ted Lilly outduels Pedro
8/24	at Toronto	5-4	2nd	-6.5	Mirabelli hits a go-ahead three-run homer in 6th
8/25	at Toronto	11-5	2nd	-5.5	Ortiz homers twice for Schilling
8/26	Detroit	4-1	2nd	-5.5	Arroyo allows less than 4 earned runs for 11th time
8/27	Detroit	5-3	2nd	-5.5	Derek Lowe goes 8 innings for the win
8/28	Detroit	5-1	2nd	-5.5	Pedro moves into top-20 on career strikeout list.
8/29	Detroit	6-1	2nd	-4.5	Tim Wakefield completes 4-game sweep
8/31	Anaheim	10-7	2nd	-3.5	Ramirez passes Jim Rice with 383 career HRs

SEPTEMBER

DATE	OPPONENT	SCORE	PLACE	GAMES BEHIND	THE SKINNY
9/1	Anaheim	12-7	2nd	-3.5	Millar homers as division title comes into sight
9/2	Anaheim	4-3	2nd	-3.5	Sox take control of wild-card race
9/3	Texas	2-0	2nd	-2.5	Martinez allows four hits in seven innings
9/4	Texas	8-6	2nd	-2.5	Streak ends as Michael Young hits a 3-run homer
9/5	Texas	6-5	2nd	-2.5	No. 35 by Ortiz backs Schilling
9/6	at Oakland	8-3	2nd	-2.5	It's some defense by Ramirez for hot Sox
9/7	at Oakland	7-1	2nd	-2.5	Lowe gets 5th straight win
9/8	at Oakland	8-3	2nd	-2	Pedro allows two hits in six innings
9/9	at Seattle	7-1	2nd	-3.5	Rookie Bobby Madritsch shuts down the Sox
9/10	at Seattle	13-2	2nd	-2.5	Schilling first pitcher to win 19 games this year
9/11	at Seattle	9-0	2nd	-2.5	Arroyo pitches seven shutout innings

DATE	OPPONENT	SCORE	PLACE	GAMES BEHIND	THE SKINNY
9/12	at Seattle	2-0	2nd	-3.5	Gil Meche pitches a five-hit shutout
9/14	Tampa Bay	5-2	2nd	-4	Rookie Scott Kazmir outduels Pedro
9/15	Tampa Bay	8-6	2nd	-4	Kevin Millar and Bellhorn hit 2-run homers
9/16	Tampa Bay	11-4	2nd	-3.5	Sox score at least 9 for the 5th time for Schilling
9/17	at NY Yankees	3-2	2nd	-2.5	Cabrera and Damon beat Mariano Rivera in 9th
9/18	at NY Yankees	14-4	2nd	-3.5	Jon Lieber a surprise star for NY
9/19	at NY Yankees	11-1	2nd	-4.5	Mike Mussina too strong
9/20	Baltimore	9-6	2nd	-4.5	Wakefield loses control in 5-run 4th
9/21	Baltimore	3-2	2nd	-4.5	Walkoff winners: Bellhorn hits 2-run single
9/22	Baltimore	7-6	2nd	-3.5	Another walkoff: Cabrera homers in the 12th
9/23	Baltimore	9-7	2nd	-4.5	Almost walkoff: Ortiz shot caught at the track
9/24	NY Yankees	6-4	2nd	-5.5	Pedro tires in the 8th (again)
9/25	NY Yankees	12-5	2nd	-4.5	Coming back with a rout
9/26	NY Yankees	11-4	2nd	-3.5	Schilling:1 hit in 7 innings
9/27	at Tampa Bay	7-3	2nd	-3	Playoff berth clinched with Manny's 43d homer
9/28	at Tampa Bay	10-8	2nd	-2.5	Millar's two-out, two-run homer in 11th wins it
9/29	at Tampa Bay	9-4	2nd	-4	Pedro loses his fourth straight

OCTOBER

DATE	OPPONENT	SCORE	PLACE	GAMES BEHIND	THE SKINNY
10/1	at Baltimore	8-3	2nd	-3.5	Damon and Ortiz give Wakefield 12th win
10/2	at Baltimore	7-5	2nd	-2	Subs are enough for win
10/2	at Baltimore	7-5	2nd	-2	Cabrera homers for a sweep
10/3	at Baltimore	3-2	2nd	-3	Scott Williamson tagged for the loss

The Red Sox were a band

of individuals as they were

seen from the outside. But

inside the clubhouse and on

the field, they came together

as the best team in baseball.

47 38 34 24 45 18 GM 5

FRANCONA

By JACKIE MACMULLAN

No glory, just guts

He wished he could sleep soundly, because the interview the following morning was important to Terry Francona. Very important. He tried to lie down, hoping to minimize the searing pain in his chest, but when he did, his breathing became shallow and labored, so he bolted upright in his Seattle hotel room in the fall of 2002, alternately frightened and disgusted. As a sharper, more insistent pain jabbed his arm, he began to doubt how he was going to get through the night.

"I was thinking, 'Aw, you've got to be kidding,' " Francona said. "I came all the way out here to have a heart attack? I should have just done that at home."

He contemplated driving himself to the hospital, but he quickly noticed that as long as he sat up, the pain diminished and his breathing improved. So he paced all night, sleepless in Seattle, revisiting his strategy to become the next manager of the Mariners.

"I was restless, so I did something that probably wasn't that smart," Francona said. "I went to work out. I rode the bike, did some push-ups. I got to the interview an hour and a half early, because I ran out of things to do."

By the time he sat down opposite Mariners president Pat Gillick, the pressure in Francona's chest was mounting. He hoped Gillick didn't notice his wiping away the sweat that kept collecting on his forehead. Could Gillick tell that Francona was actually gasping for air between sentences?

There was something wrong, no doubt about that. Francona hadn't felt right since he underwent arthroscopic surgery the previous week to clean out particles and fragments in both knees, unwanted souvenirs of a 10-year major league career diminished by two grisly injuries. He had learned to fight through pain, the kind that required 8 to 10 rolls of tape every game just to hobble onto the field.

He needed to fight through this, too. Francona couldn't pass on this opportunity with Seattle. He had interviewed days earlier for the manager's position with the New York Mets and it had gone fine, but not so fine that Francona felt he had the job. He missed baseball. He missed it desperately, even after the fans in Philadelphia had booed and mocked him, slashed his tires and crossed the street with the express purpose of insulting him. He lost 97 games in his final season as the Phillies' manager in 2000, but that was nothing compared to the humiliation of being told his services were no longer needed. He knew what he was doing. Why did they give up on him?

"I didn't understand how much I loved the game until it was taken away from me," Francona acknowledged. "It killed me not to be in baseball."

Yet his efforts to return to the game nearly killed him as well.

The new manager of the Boston Red Sox cheated death four times during a medical odyssey that included multiple knee surgeries, blood clots, staph infections, massive internal bleeding, and a near amputation of his leg. Francona was so ill during the Christmas of 2002, the mere thought of managing a baseball team was ludicrous. Within weeks of his interview in Seattle, he was hospitalized in intensive care, fighting for his life.

50

NUMBER OF
PLAYERS ON
ROSTER
DURING
REGULAR
SEASON

"Looking back, Pat Gillick must have thought I was nuts," Francona said. "I had to ask him to repeat questions a couple of times. I was really struggling."

"He interviewed all day, half dead," said his wife, Jacque Francona, who is a nurse. "He was supposed to meet an old friend for dinner, but he couldn't even walk the two blocks to the restaurant."

"I'm probably lucky to be alive," said Francona, in his first extensive comments regarding his ordeal. "And I know I'm lucky to have all my limbs."

Sixteen months later, Terry Francona is feeling fine, full of energy and ideas on Nomar vs. A-Rod, the acquisition of Curt Schilling, the signing of Keith Foulke, and the handling of Manny Ramirez.

He already has been compartmentalized as a player's manager, and the Fenway Faithful wonder aloud whether he has the guts to stand up to superstars Pedro Martinez and Ramirez.

"After all he's been through," said Brad Mills, who will be Francona's bench coach in Boston, "how can anyone question his toughness? They'll see."

They'll see. Ask former Philadelphia pitcher Bobby Munoz and current Phillies outfielder Bobby Abreu whether Francona has the courage to enforce his will in a major league clubhouse.

When Francona took the Phillies job in 1997, he inherited a veteran pitching staff that included Schilling and Andy Ashby. He also inherited a young catcher named Mike Lieberthal.

"In the beginning, Lieberthal didn't always put down the right fingers," said Mills, who was on Francona's staff. "He was learning on the go. Some of the older pitchers got frustrated with him."

After a particularly rough outing, Munoz, a young, impressionable pitcher swayed by the private complaints of his elders, savaged his catcher in the newspapers. The next day, he was summoned to the manager's office.

"Terry left the door cracked open," said Rico Brogna, who played on that team. "He wanted us to hear everything. He called out Munoz without embarrassing him in front of his teammates, yet by leaving that door open, he made sure we all got the message.

"We sat there wide-eyed, our jaws dropping. No one had ever heard Terry shout like that. I'm sure he looked out and thought, 'Mission accomplished.' "

Francona's message to his players was succinct: I'll fight for you, as long as you follow my rules. Abreu, an outfielder with a sweet swing, tested Francona's patience by arriving late to the park. The first time, the manager ushered him into his office and calmly explained tardiness was unacceptable. The second time, the player was fined. The third time, Francona threw Abreu out of the clubhouse.

"Terry wanted to send Bobby home, but the ball club wouldn't let him," Mills said. "Even though the front office wouldn't stand behind him, Terry still found a way to make it work. He stayed on Bobby. He made him a better player."

Last season, Abreu batted .300, hit 20 homers, knocked in 101 runs, and stole 22 bases for Philly. Lieberthal, who became an All-Star in 1999, batted .313 with 81 RBIs. Francona's imprints remain on both players, even if his record in Philadelphia (285-363 in four seasons) indicates a failed mission. Truth is, his job was doomed from the outset. The fans wanted favorite son Larry Bowa, and they got him — but only after Francona absorbed the blows of a rebuilding process.

"We were a young team that wasn't going to be very good," said Lee Thomas, who hired Francona. "I wanted a guy that could handle adversity."

Francona proved to be adept at that. When his face appeared on the Jumbotron at a Sixers game shortly after he was hired, he was instantly booed. Francona smiled and waved anyway. He didn't flinch when a group of malcontents slashed his tires on Fan Appreciation Day. He jokingly offered to draw straws with his staff when one of his relievers was getting shelled and he had to make that long trek to the mound to absorb the ire of the crowd.

"He was excellent at alleviating the pressure on the team," said Mills. "He took it all, and put it on himself."

"You learn to live with it," Francona said. "You learn to be tough in a hurry."

He could tough out almost anything. But by the time Francona had taken his red-eye flight from Seattle to Baltimore in the fall of 2002, he was sweating profusely, and his chest felt like it was going to explode. He went directly to the emergency room and underwent tests. He waited for a diagnosis. Instead, they sent him home.

He went to his daughter Alyssa's volleyball game, but the pain in his chest persisted. He still could not lie down. He still could not sleep. The next morning, Francona's physician called and ordered him to return to the hospital as soon as possible.

The X-rays had revealed a pulmonary embolism on each side of his lungs. He was admitted for four days and was sent home with blood thinners to avoid future clotting.

"They told me I was lucky," Francona said.

Yet, within days, Francona's surgically repaired knees began to ache. He stood on the sideline at his daughter Jamie's soccer game, fighting nausea from the incessant throbbing. That night, Francona was back at the hospital.

"They were trying to determine the extent of his problems by using a pain scale," said Jacque. "They'd ask him how much it hurt on a scale of 1 to 10. Terry would say, 'Oh, about a 5.'

"I kept telling them his pain scale was different from other people. A '5' for Terry was a '12' for other people."

It took two surgeries on each knee to eliminate the infection. Francona felt as though he had been leveled by a train. He couldn't understand why he felt so sluggish, and why, two days before his scheduled discharge, he still couldn't walk properly. The morning he was supposed to leave, he requested another examination. Within hours, he was back in emergency surgery, this time for massive internal bleeding in his right thigh. He suffered from compartment syndrome, an extremely painful condition that occurs when pressure within the muscles builds to dangerous levels, and prevents nourishment from reaching nerve and muscle cells. Those cells can die within a matter of hours. Because his surgeon identified the problem quickly, she not only saved his leg, she saved Francona's life — for the third time.

When Tito Francona called to check on his son, who days earlier had downplayed his illness, he was alarmed by the report he received from Jacque.

"I said to my wife, 'We better go see

him,' " Tito said. "It was awful. They had his leg sliced open. They had all this netting in there to prevent the clotting. Terry has always been able to withstand a lot of pain, but he was having a tough time with that one."

Tito Francona played 15 years in the majors, and from the time Terry could toddle alongside his father, he ran errands for Al Downing, played catch with outfielder Tom Reynolds, went fishing with Phil Niekro. Terry knew Dad's mantra: Behave, and you can come. Slip up, and you stay home.

"I think I only had to leave him behind once," Tito said. "He loved being at the park. And it gave him a great advantage. I remember the first time I walked into Yankee Stadium. It was like, 'Whoa.' Very intimidating. But by the time Terry started playing, he had already seen it all."

Francona earned a scholarship to Arizona and showed up wearing cutoffs and hair down to his shoulders. He immediately took it upon himself to assign nicknames to almost every player on the team. He was a smart hitter who batted .401 with 84 RBIs in his junior season and was named the MVP of the College World Series. He was the 22d pick of the Montreal Expos in 1980 and was on his way to stardom when he caught his cleat on the warning track at Busch Stadium chasing down a fly ball in '82. Jacque, back in Montreal at catcher Gary Carter's house for a birthday party, glanced at the television to see her husband wheeled off the field on a stretcher.

The rehabilitation was brutal. Francona made his trainer lay on top of his leg to create resistance. He threw balled-up socks back and forth to his wife to improve his balance and flexibility. It was a grueling comeback, but within two seasons, he was almost like new, whacking the cover off the ball again, before he hurt his other knee running out a ground ball. Another major surgery. Another excruciating rehab. He was never the same. The would-be superstar was reduced to being a reliable pinch hitter.

"But I never once got surprised in that role," Francona said. "I was ready every night, every at-bat."

When he stopped playing after 10 seasons, he went directly into coaching. He was a tornado of energy, enthusiastic and

"After all he's been through," said Brad Mills, who will be Francona's bench coach in Boston, "how can anyone question his toughness? They'll see."

47

COME-FROM-
BEHIND
VICTORIES IN 2004
REGULAR SEASON

17-12

RECORD IN
GAMES DECIDED IN
THE LAST
AT BAT

88-1

RECORD WHEN
LEADING
AFTER EIGHT
INNINGS

infected with a passion for baseball.

"He was always on the move," said Thomas. "A very high-energy guy."

But by the time Francona was released from the hospital late in November 2002, the life had been sucked out of his body. It was a chore for him to move from his bed to the couch. He was listless, despondent.

"He never had any strength," Jacque said. "The bathroom was 8 feet away, and he couldn't get there."

Between Thanksgiving and Dec. 11 of that year, Francona ventured downstairs only twice. He was too tired and too sick to even bother to ask if anyone from Seattle or New York had ever called back.

His family and friends were worried. Where was the old Terry? Where was the playful, fun-loving guy who embraced life with both arms outstretched?

"When I started dating him in college," Jacque said, "I would be walking on campus, and he'd see me and tackle me on the grass."

One morning, that same man, in a deadened voice she hardly recognized, told her he wanted to go back to the hospital. Jacque said she'd pull up the car. Terry told her to call an ambulance instead.

"That's when I knew we were in trouble," Jacque said.

Francona had suffered massive clotting. The Greenfield filter saved his life by trapping the clots, but, as a result, the filter became severely clogged, and prevented a healthy blood supply from reaching his arteries. Doctors explained he would now have to work on improving his collateral circulation, a process in which smaller arteries open and serve as alternate routes of blood supply to the larger arteries. They told Francona a full recovery was rare. They told him he might always walk with a limp.

Francona would never jog again. He tried to swing a bat and was exhausted after two tries. Climbing stairs was a major endeavor. He was supposed to report as Ken Macha's new bench coach for Oakland in late February, but it became apparent that was an unrealistic goal.

"He called me up with about two weeks left until spring training," Macha said. "He said, 'I know you've been waiting a long time to manage a big-league team, and I don't want to screw that up for you. I'm not myself. I can't even throw batting

practice. You better get someone else.'

"I told him, 'Terry, I didn't hire you to throw batting practice. I hired you to be around our team, to let us pick your brain. I hired you because your demeanor is so positive, it can't help but rub off on people.'"

Francona got better in time. He'd work with the players, then retreat home and nap for hours. Eventually, his strength returned. His muscles began responding. By the time Oakland met the Red Sox in the postseason, he was bounding out to the mound for BP and concocting nicknames for the A's.

When Boston decided not to renew Grady Little's contract, Francona was one of the first people Sox general manager Theo Epstein called, in part because of his "positive energy."

"I had a really favorable impression of him after our interview," said Epstein, "but I had one major concern: Was he too nice? This is a team full of superstars, and if the manager is too nice, and doesn't know where and when to draw the line, that was going to be a problem.

"But then we looked into Terry's background, heard some of the stories, and came away very satisfied."

Asked for specific examples of what he learned, Esptein laughed, then said, "We heard about some epic snaps. Terry knows how to yell and scream at the right times."

He does not favor superstars. He established that back in 1994, when he managed the Double A Birmingham Barons and Michael Jordan was one of his outfielders. Jordan, constantly flummoxed by curveballs, had struck out four times in a row when he was due to bat in the ninth of a close game. Francona pinch hit for him. Naturally, one of the greatest athletic competitors of all-time was bitterly disappointed, but Francona needed a win, and he was pretty certain a basketball star batting .190 wasn't going to deliver it for him.

"Michael knew where I stood on things," Francona said. "In one of his first games, he popped the ball up and just stood there. I waited for him to come in, and I said, 'Are you going to do that every time? Tell me now.' He looked at me and said, 'Never again. I promise.'"

"If guys don't hustle, Terry will go crazy no matter who it is," Brogna predicted. "He won't have any trouble letting a guy like Manny [Ramirez] know what he expects. He'll make Manny responsible for his own behavior."

"He won't be afraid to pull any guy out of a ballgame," said Thomas. "Not just pitchers. Anyone who doesn't do the things that Terry feels will help the team win."

The Boston tenure of Terry Francona will begin in earnest. Few will notice him wince when he ambles up those dugout steps; the burning in his legs when he climbs stairs is one of the permanent reminders of his surreal medical nightmare.

"If that's the worst of it, then I'll take it," he said. "I can still get on the treadmill. I can hit BP all day. It will not affect how I manage the team."

His team is the Boston Red Sox. His job is to win the World Series. His passion is the game of baseball, and all the sleepless nights that come with it. ☻

TERRY FRANCONA WASN'T AFRAID TO PULL PITCHERS AT ANY TIME

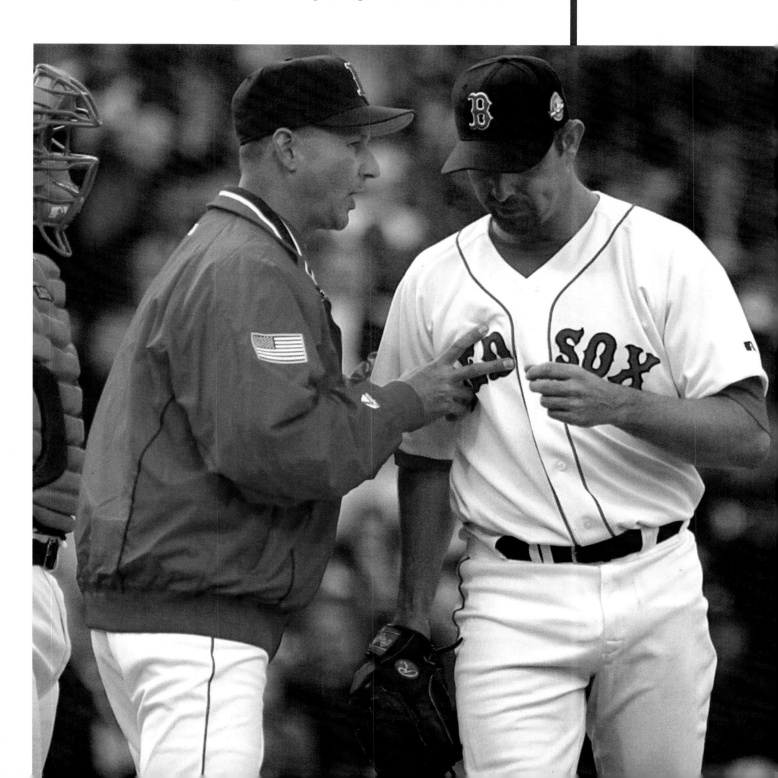

SCHILLING

CURT

By GORDON EDES

New ace

This midday visit in the desert with Curt Schilling, sitting in baggy shorts and a Semper Fi Marine T-shirt on an ornate sofa in front of the lavish bronze curtains that decorate his den in Scottsdale, Ariz., along with the awards he has collected through the years, is just a tiny slice of his nonstop dialogue with the world. The one in which there's no telling whom he'll speak with next, in a voice he claims is Everyman's but tends to be heard more because of who he is, one of the best pitchers in baseball.

They've all fallen within range of that voice:

His father, Master Sergeant Cliff Schilling, who died just before his son made it to the big leagues but had told him at age 13 he would someday get there.

His wife, Shonda, who challenged him to take his game to a higher level, then locked her hands inside his in a fight against melanoma that after five surgeries has her cancer-free but ever-vigilant.

Roger Clemens, who pulled him aside during an offseason workout in the Astrodome and lectured him at an early age that he was foolish to waste the precious gift he had.

Greg Maddux, the pitching master from whom Schilling took his cue on how to approach his craft, which led him to amass a digital video library of more than 30,000 disks of every batter

21-6

2004
REGULAR
SEASON
RECORD

3.26

REGULAR
SEASON
ERA

12-1

RECORD AT
FENWAY PARK
DURING
REGULAR
SEASON

he has ever faced.

Bob Gibson, the pitching grandmaster with whom Schilling traded hours of shop talk about high-velocity fastballs and a shared thirst for competition.

Randy Johnson, the Arizona ace with whom Schilling shared the Most Valuable Player award during the 2001 World Series and who says Schilling eased his burden of being the ace of a staff that won it all with two pitchers of the highest caliber. Sixteen times that championship season, they pitched on back-to-back days, and not once on those occasions did the D-Backs lose consecutive games. In a hallway off the den, there's a portrait of Schilling and Johnson holding their MVP awards, weary but joyous.

Theo Epstein, the Red Sox general manager sitting at his Thanksgiving table, setting aside for the moment his goal of persuading Schilling to accept a trade to the Red Sox to accept another helping of stuffing.

Bill James, the Sox statman who sent Schilling urging him to come to Boston. Schilling said he was 14 when he figured out one of James's principal tenets, that on-base percentage was a lot more important than batting average.

The fighter pilot who was diagnosed with ALS, Lou Gehrig's disease, during the Gulf War, who came to Fenway Park a couple of years ago and saw Schilling, who has made it a big part of his life work to support ALS research, outduel Sox ace Pedro Martinez on national TV.

The radio talk-show hosts in Philadelphia who so annoyed Schilling that he would call them on his way to the ballpark to argue with them.

The emergency workers at Ground Zero who were deeply moved by the words a shaken but proud Schilling delivered at the site just a couple of weeks after Sept. 11, the same player who urged all big-leaguers in an eloquent letter to donate a day's pay to the victims of that tragedy.

The guys on the Internet baseball chat boards, with log-ons like GodSamGod and Spaceman's Bong, shocked to find in the middle of the night that the "gehrig38" who was updating them about the Schilling negotiations was Schilling himself.

His son, Gehrig, who came home from school after the trade and said, "Daddy, do you know what a snow day is? It's when it snows so much they have no school. They have snow days in Boston!"

Schilling, with $12 million due him next year in the last year of his Arizona contract, knew the team would ask him to waive his no-trade clause and accept a deal to another team. Initially, he had only two teams in mind — the Yankees, who he thought gave him the best chance to win another Series ring — and the Phillies, the team he'd pitched to the '93 Series, in a city where he plans to make his offseason home. But when Terry Francona, the former Phillies manager and a good friend, emerged as the front-runner for the Sox job, Schilling said he went to the D-Backs and told them that he would consider Boston, too.

Schilling is coming here to win. Just look at his contract: He has the usual performance bonuses for achieving personal honors, such the Cy Young Award or an All-Star nod. That money is earmarked for charity. He also has a clause that calls for a $2 million bonus (plus a bump in his base salary) if the Sox win the World Series during the course of the next three years, and guarantees the option on the 2007 season. (The option also kicks in, he says, if he makes 90 starts and pitches 600 innings over the life of the contract, or pitches 200 innings and makes 30 starts in the last year of the deal.)

So Schilling was motivated to make sure there would not be extraneous stuff standing between him and winning in October.

"I had heard extensive rumors about the Boston clubhouse," he said. "There were issues I wanted to talk to the Red Sox about, and I talked to them about it. I'm pretty confident I'm walking into a situation that will be a lot of fun.

"They know there needs to be enough muscle, personalitywise, that clubhouse stuff doesn't affect on-the-field performance in a negative way."

Schilling expects to bring some of that muscle, not so much to the everyday players ("I can't even fathom the grind they go through") but to the pitching staff.

"I can certainly be a large factor that the 10-to-12 man staff is as tight-knit a group as it can be," he said. "When I talked to Pedro, I was clear to him about a lot of things, and that was one of the things. I can't wait to pitch with him."

It shouldn't be hard to figure out which day is Schilling's to pitch. For one thing, he wears the same ensemble to the park — one his wife and kids choose for him in spring training — every time he pitches. Luis Gonzalez, Arizona's All-Star outfielder, threatened to burn Schilling's clothes after one season.

In that sense, Schilling has something in common with Nomar Garciaparra: a devotion to routine that does not vary.

"Mentally, I try to put myself in a place I can only get to once every five days," he said. "The only difference between my first start in spring training and my last start in the World Series is the game itself.

"I think if you have integrity, if you have pride, if you have respect for your teammates and the game, some sort of routine will develop naturally, because nobody just shows up and plays and does well for an extended period of time."

Fear of failure, he says, is a great motivator, and his pregame preparation reflects an attention to detail that very few pitchers approach. From Maddux, he said, he learned that the key to preparation is understanding when a hitter is going to swing at a pitch and when he is going to take one.

"Once you understand that," he said, "the key is throwing a strike when he's taking and a ball when he's swinging. It can be done. Hitters are creatures of habit. They do things on certain counts and in certain situations that they don't in other counts and in other situations. For a freakin' $13 million a year, is it too much to ask me to know when that is?"

Tony Gwynn, the future Hall of Famer from the San Diego Padres, inspired Schilling to amass his video library. Schilling was due to pitch against the Padres the night after Gwynn had five hits in a game. As he lay in bed, Schilling said, he was frustrated at the thought that Gwynn, a passionate student of pitching, knew exactly what Schilling planned to do the next day. Schilling decided that imitation was the highest form of flattery, and like Gwynn, he amassed a video library of every game he was in.

"I can break it down any way I want," he said. "I can pull up Andres Galarraga's at-bats against me and break them down by count, by pitch selection, pitch location, pitch result — whatever I want to look at."

During games, it is not unusual to see Schilling position his fielders. They go along with it, because the results speak for themselves.

Even at 37, Schilling doesn't expect those results to change. At the outset of every season, his goals are to make 35 starts and pitch 245 innings, which averages to seven innings a start. No six innings and out for him.

"I've always felt as a starting pitcher that your reputation is made after the sixth inning," he said, "and what you do in the seventh, eighth, and ninth innings facing guys for a third or fourth time. That is really an in-depth look at how good you are.

"Top-of-the-rotation guys are not six-inning guys. Top-of-the-rotation guys, you're paying them (a) to win games and (b) to pitch innings. Nothing can be done without pitching innings. If you pitch your innings, and if you have the talent, all your other numbers will fall in place."

It is as much a part of Schilling's game to be heard as it is to be seen, for which he makes no apologies. His wife once said she never realized how much his teammates had to listen to until she rode the team plane on a family trip and heard for herself.

Schilling will challenge a reporter or columnist who he believes has been unfair, and like his post-midnight Net chats, will make some direct connections to the fans.

"People get the idea that we're different human beings than they are," he said. "I don't think anything can be further from the truth. In some ways, we're a lot more like them than anyone wants to believe."

He's already planning to recruit Sox fans for "Curt's Pitch for ALS," in which he donates $100 a strikeout and $100 a win three times over — once each for the Philadelphia, Arizona, and now the Boston chapter of the ALS Society. He invites fans to donate from $1 to $10 per win and strikeout, then invites them all to a party at the end of the season.

"I'm living a dream. Sometimes I'm scared it's too good at times." ☺

"People get the idea that we're different human beings than they are," Schilling said. "I don't think anything can be further from the truth. In some ways, we're a lot more like them than anyone wants to believe."

ORTIZ

DAVID

DESIGNATED
HITTER

34

By JACKIE MACMULLEN

Green light

He knew he had this in him, from the time he was a little boy in bare feet in the Dominican, yearning to play shortstop, dreaming of becoming an NBA star, fantasizing about crushing home runs out of major league parks.

Some dreams simply don't come true. Other dreams merely have to wait.

When David Ortiz finally made it to the big leagues full-time in 2000, he dutifully took orders from a manager, Tom Kelly, who urged him to concentrate on base hits, not Babe Ruth swings. Just four short years ago, Boston's indefatigable slugger was a singles hitter for the Minnesota Twins, batting (.282) with only 10 home runs in 130 games.

"Something with my swing was not right in Minnesota," Ortiz said. "I could never hit for power. Whenever I took a big swing, they'd say to me, 'Hey, hey, what are you doing?' So I said, 'You want me to hit like a little bitch, then I will.'"

"But I knew I could hit for power. It was just a matter of getting the green light."

There were times he would leave the park frustrated and angry. He did not like that feeling. He was a proud man, but one who vowed never to become spoiled or greedy or selfish. He came from the same country where his friend Pedro Martinez sat under the mango tree and wondered how he'd scrape up 50 cents to catch a bus. David Ortiz was a happy, grateful person. Baseball had afforded him a life he could only dream of, and he would not let the disappointments of a simple game overtake him.

In the winter of 2002, he became a free agent. His employer, the Twins, expressed tepid interest. The Boston Red Sox signed the big lefthander for a relatively modest fee (one-year, $1.25 million), slightly outbidding the New York Yankees.

"In my first at-bat at spring training, there was a man on first," Ortiz said. "I tried to move the runner over. When I got to the dugout, [manager] Grady Little said, 'Hey, hey, you got to bring that guy in.' I said, 'OK, I guess I've got the green light to swing.'"

His swing has been refined by hitting coach Ron Jackson, who made minor adjustments with his elbow, his choke on the bat, and his timing. He told Ortiz to wait as long as he possibly could before he swung. He talked about "loading up," utilizing the strength of his sturdy, 6-foot-4-inch, 230-pound frame to its maximum.

"Think of what it's like to get ready to throw a punch," Papa Jack said. "If you really want to hit somebody hard, you've got to draw back. That's what I mean by loading up. That's what we had David work on."

You want loading up? Here's what Ortiz piled on the Yankees in the American League Championship Series: A .387 average, 3 home runs, 11 RBIs, 23 total bases, a slugging percentage of (.742), an on-base percentage of (.457), and an MVP trophy for a walkoff home run and a walkoff single that have propelled him into national stardom.

"It's ridiculous," said teammate Doug Mientkiewicz. "It's gotten to the point where he swings with such conviction, he doesn't even need to be hitting a strike anymore."

When the St. Louis Cardinals jog onto the emerald lawn of Fenway Park to-

night for Game 1 of the World Series, you can be sure of one thing: They will do everything they can not to let Ortiz beat them.

"But the way he's hitting, it might not matter what they do," said Jackson.

Ortiz's incredible hitting display has drawn comparisons to the original Mr. October, Reggie Jackson, as well as former Red Sox outfielder Dave Henderson, whose dramatic clutch hits in 1986 made him an instant folk hero.

"Once you get into a groove like that, you feel invincible," said Henderson. "I feel like I could hit anybody, and the opposing team could sense that. When you make a pitcher nervous on the mound, they end up trying to throw around you, or making a mistake, and it usually helps out the hitter."

Henderson, not unlike Ortiz, was a congenial personality who seemed impervious to pressure.

"The guys that get nervous are the guys who go 0 for 5," Henderson said. "David and I have that big smile in common. But the big difference is Ortiz isn't sneaking up on anybody. He's the No. 5 hitter. I was batting seventh or eighth.

"Pitchers go into the game worrying about Ortiz hurting them, and he goes out and does it anyway."

He has been so good you wonder if it's really as easy as it looks, but then, you don't see Ortiz retreat between innings to the clubhouse so he can rewind the video of his previous at-bat. When you are the designated hitter, you have that luxury.

"We were sitting in the clubhouse during Game 7 [of the ACLS]," revealed outfielder Gabe Kapler. "It was about the third inning. I'm stretching, trying to get ready. I was telling him how impressed I was that Curt Schilling still gets nervous before a big game. I told him I thought it was amazing a guy of his caliber still has the jitters.

"David looks at me and says, 'I never get nervous.'

"Now my first inclination was not to believe him. But he says, 'When I start feeling that way, I think about what I've gone through in my life, and then I put things in the proper place.' By prioritizing baseball, it allowed him to be at ease, and to relax.

"It shows on the field. There is always this calmness about him. And when pitchers see that calmness, I think it worries them."

You must go back to the Dominican, to sultry summer days when Ortiz begged to play shortstop, even though he was a lefty; when he saw Michael Jordan play on TV, and decided he wanted to be like Mike; when the pitches he saw appeared as big as beach balls, to understand this simple life is what prevents him from

91

2004 REGULAR
SEASON
EXTRA-BASE HITS,
BEST IN AL

139

REGULAR
SEASON
RBIS

.301

REGULAR
SEASON
BATTING
AVERAGE

allowing baseball to be complicated. He was poor, but so were his neighbors, his friends, and his relatives. His parents loved him and educated him, and that was enough. As Ortiz so aptly explained it himself, "Growing up in the Dominican ain't easy, but it ain't bad, either.

"I always think back to where I came from," he said. "I never forget about that. I was down in Jamaica Plain the other day. They have a lot of people from my hometown in the Dominican living there.

"I went to the barber shop to get a haircut, and there was no one in there. A half an hour later, the people were in the streets, waiting for me to come out of the barber shop.

"My friend asked me, 'How come you aren't like the basketball players?' The other day one of them came into this club and no one got close to him, because he had three bodyguards with him. People just wanted to try and say, 'Hey, good job,' or 'What's up? Can I have an autograph?' People don't want to hurt you. They just want to say hello.

"The people [from the barber shop], they see me all the time in the Dominican. If I come out with three bodyguards, how can they talk to me? There is no reason for that."

The lasting image for most of America is Ortiz's mighty swing, and the havoc it wreaked on the Yankees. It has brought him new respect in the form of phone calls from Jordan, rock star receptions in Boston, unsolicited advice from Reggie Jackson.

"I was talking to him about hitting three home runs in one game in the World Series," Ortiz said. "He said pitchers back then had heart. They weren't afraid to come right after you. I told him, 'I guess pitchers now are smart.'"

"David is the first guy I've seen who would go 0 for 5 with three strikeouts and come on the bus and say, 'It's OK, someone is going to pay tomorrow,'" said Mientkiewicz. "And, 99 percent of the time, he'd do something great the next day."

"He's been in a zone all year," said Jackson. "The concentration is the main thing. He's having all good at-bats. He's hitting the ball to left field, right field and up the middle."

All he needed was the green light. ☺

"It's ridiculous," said teammate Doug Mientkiewicz. "It's gotten to the point where he swings with such conviction, he doesn't even need to be hitting a strike anymore."

TOTAL LUNAR ECLIPSE

OCTOBER 27, 2004 | 10:25 P.M.